THE HORSE
THAT HAUNTS
MY HEART

The Horse That Haunts My Heart

Deborah Smith Parker

Astrologicus Press

Cover photo, Teri Rider.
Cover design, interior design and typography, Teri Rider.

Library of Congress Control Number: 2014940249

Astrologicus Press
P.O. Box 722757
San Diego, California 92172
www.astrologicuspress.com

Printed in USA

DEDICATION

For anyone who loved a horse—or wished they had one to love.

Acknowledgments

I am indebted to those who reviewed my manuscript in its various stages of development and for their valuable feedback: Hatheway Brooks, Jill Estensen, Karen Hawthorne, Jim Hennum, Nancy Maples, Nancy Plaxico, Diane Rhodes, and Marjhe Tannler.

I am grateful to Deb Flemming and her years of newspaper editing skills she surgically applied to my manuscript that helped to better shape the telling of my story. I am indebted to Beth Escott Newcomer for her suggestions to explain "why" in all the places I kept too much in memory and didn't put enough on the pages.

I deeply appreciate the work and dedication of my talented and supportive colleague and friend Teri Rider who designed the cover and interior layout, managed the production end of this book, and coached me through the prolonged and intense labor we writers go through to deliver a completed manuscript.

I want to thank all the horse lovers who have encouraged me every step of the way to get this remarkable story out of my head and heart and into a form they can read.

Finally, I'm grateful to my husband, Jeff, for understanding the importance of this book to me and—as he has for over 30 years—supporting me in his many surprising and wondrous Aquarian ways.

CONTENTS

PREFACE

This is the story of the most extraordinary horse I have ever known and how I came to know that about him. At first glance he didn't appear extraordinary. His Clark Kent exterior made it easy to dismiss him. I made that mistake when we met more than 50 years ago on a ranch in the West.

This story is also about more than him and me, but without him there would be no story—for he is the keystone in the archway I passed through to bring what happened to book form.

A story isn't just a narration of events and anecdotes. Oh, it's full of those things, but they aren't what make it stick in the mind and haunt the heart. The elements of a story must first be stuck in the writer's mind, haunt the writer's heart, those fragments of events or feelings too big or too complicated to fully understand at the time they happened. So there they stay, hidden under the smooth covers of the stories we tell ourselves, living half-lives isolated in hollows of the soul. But like sand within an oyster, they are what eventually make the pearl of the story grow.

Our psyches work tirelessly to complete what is left unfinished, finding ways to eventually rescue those long-hidden fragments and reintroduce them to each other, bringing them, finally, into right relationship.

This is when the work of the writer begins, and this is how the true story is discovered. And that story *always* surprises the writer.

Robert Frost said about the writing process, "No tears for the writer, no tears for the reader. No surprise for the writer, no surprise for the reader."

I found plenty of both writing this book, some of which I'll tell here— and they won't be spoilers for the reader:

I was amazed that so many seemingly unrelated, but impactful, intersecting events with long and powerful reaches into my future occurred in the relatively brief period of my life in which this story took place.

I was surprised that only a handful of people crossed the very long bridge in time to claim their places as main characters. I ultimately had to bow to the decisions of those I also considered to be important in my life at the time but who simply refused my efforts to put them in the spotlight, choosing instead to remain unnamed extras hovering on the outskirts of the main action. This bewildered me since they were not fictional characters I was creating to advance the story line—they were real people with whom I shared actual events.

It was also surprising to me that among the large cast of people involved in the events of this story I could only remember the names of a few, and that I could not place the names or recall the faces of several who were with me during some of the most intense episodes described in this book.

I really struggled with the fact that my best friend at home, who came to the ranch with me my first summer, couldn't be coaxed into the story at all except for a cameo appearance at the very end.

I never could have imagined the constellation of events 50 years later that would initiate the download of memories that compelled me to write this story.

However, my biggest surprise was to see revealed my horse's life-long contributions to my understanding and healing of my relationship patterns with men—and to say more about that here would indeed be a spoiler.

Just like the rugged mountains in which these events took place, this story has rapidly shifting light and shadow. That is why I chose to change the names of both horses and people and to be intentionally vague about the location of the ranch—to protect the innocent and by unfortunate extension, the guilty.

Chapter 1

My Dream

Horses, horses, horses

I always wanted a horse more than I wanted anything. Mom and Dad did not wear down easily on this issue—in fact, they didn't wear down at all. They made it clear they were not getting me a horse but they would, they assured me, make sure I had access to horses. They kept their word, arranging for me to ride at local stables and during regular visits to family friends who had horses. In the summers I went to camp where I was able to ride several times a week.

However, I never stopped longing for a horse of my own. I just talked about it less. At night, I took that longing into my inner life, praying for dreams about horses. Actually, they weren't prayers as much as they were 911 calls from me begging to be transported in sleep to a night of riding the wind on horseback. I did this privately after the obligatory "Now I lay me down to sleep…" mechanically recited each night with my mother—and after she kissed me good night, turned off my bedroom light and left me to what I hoped would be a night full of magic on the back of a magnificent horse, its mane streaming in my face, its powerful legs thundering across the earth, sometimes carrying me up toward the stars.

I had those dreams, but not as often as I would have liked. What they lacked in frequency was compensated by their content. They were unusual in that in nearly all of them there was a point at which the horse looked me full in the face and then spoke. There was always something deep and wise in its voice and eyes. Whatever message the horse had for me was brief and surprising, but when I awoke I could never recall what it was. I was, however, able to snuggle under the covers to steal a few more precious minutes still wrapped in the intimacy I shared with the horse who had just visited me in my dream.

Meanwhile, my day dreams were assisted by my imagination creating scenarios in which I could live with horses, eventually focusing on vivid scenes encompassing an entire lifestyle—to live and breathe horses each day and to do that far from the gentrified farms, primly fenced pastures and manicured trails of the East. I wanted to run wild with horses over the rough country of the West where every day was an adventure.

Mid-way through grade school when most of my friends asked for frilly, girlie Christmas gifts, I requested and got a large ranch set. It was marvelous, providing the essentials for an entire ranch: corrals and hitching rails, a ranch house, barn and bunkhouse. The best part for me were the many horses in different action postures—rearing, running, and even the back-on-its-hind-legs-fast-stop stance a trained roping horse makes when the rider lassoes a calf and the horse slams on the brakes to keep the lariat taut.

I loved "catching" the horses, bridling and saddling them with rubber bridles and saddles that had straps and cinches I could fasten. There were cowboys I could place in the saddles but in my mind it was always me up there. My ranch remained spread out on the floor in a corner of my bedroom for a long time.

Then one afternoon in fifth grade something happened, revealing my call to the West was deeply rooted in a place and—surprising to me—a time much further away than my imagination had taken me to date.

I always watched TV westerns after school. Our local stations sometimes played western singing groups between cowboy films. Not a fan of that kind of music at the time, I usually headed for the kitchen to grab a snack—except for the day I stood rooted in front of the TV, captured by a verse that shot chills through me. I couldn't remember the exact words but it was about a cowboy saying when he died he wanted his bones tied to the back of his horse and together they'd wander the West.

Those words touched me deep in *my* bones. I began to recognize that I didn't just want to go live on a ranch sometime in the future. I also wanted to return to a place buried somewhere in my past, *someplace I already knew*, that now called to me. It was a strange feeling—being pulled out of time. And it was not the last time I would feel that way.

Oh, how I longed to be in that reality, a reality that felt so familiar.

CHAPTER 2

My Dream Comes to Life

It's happening!

Halfway through seventh grade a miracle happened. One night Dad leaned across the dinner table, trying unsuccessfully to suppress his smile, and asked if I'd be interested in going to a ranch camp the following summer. I nearly came out of my skin.

He'd been checking out several ranches in the West for a year or so but hadn't said anything to me until he found something he thought I'd like. Most ranches kept the girls on too tight a leash, he felt, and too removed from their horses, more like a dude ranch where girls have limited access to horses and no active participation in ranch operations.

At the ranch he liked and hoped I would, each girl got her own horse. The focus of the entire summer was girls and their horses living the ranching life. He said he'd talked with the ranch owner, Sam, who was currently in the Midwest to meet with the families of prospective campers. He would be available to come to our home in a couple of weeks so we could learn more. It seemed unbelievable this was happening.

When Sam came to our home he showed us reels of 8mm movies (this was the late 1950s) of the ranch and of horses and girls going all kinds of places, doing things I'd only dreamed of. I needed no selling—nor did I have to sell my parents on this. They were offering it to me!

Sam talked with both me and my parents about my experience with horses and capacities as a rider. He also wanted to get a sense of my personality so he could make a good match for me with a horse. Dad asked if a girl could switch horses if she felt she and her horse weren't a good match. Sam told us that was always an option but one rarely exercised since the normal course of events was that each girl quickly fell in love with her horse.

Heading west

The day after school was out I watched my parents wave goodbye as my train pulled out of Union Station in Chicago heading west where I would arrive more than 30 hours later and not return home for 11 weeks.

That was quite a train ride. I had traveled long distances on trains several times with my parents and we always had sleeping compartments. No such luck on this trip. We went coach—more than 40 very excited girls bouncing all over our car. Throughout the night and early morning the train stopped at other cities, picking up more girls.

Girls' camps are really big on singing, which I loved. The girls who were returning to the ranch taught us newcomers some of the songs sung there. I didn't know any of them but had at least heard a few like: "Tumbling Tumbleweeds," "Strawberry Roan," and "Let the Rest of the World Go By."

As it became dark the pace of the songs slowed and we sang those with soothing rocking rhythms and lyrics telling of riding night herd and calming cattle. It was getting late and I started to doze off. Suddenly I jerked wide-awake when I heard:

> *When I die take my saddle from the wall,*
> *Put it on my pony and lead him from the stall.*
> *Tie my bones to his back, turn our faces to the west*
> *And we'll ride the prairies that we love the best.*

That was it! That was the verse I'd heard a couple of years earlier that so stirred my soul and memory. I learned it was the last verse of "I Ride an Old Paint." Yes, I was finally returning home.

When the train arrived at our stop late the following afternoon we were still four hours from the ranch. It was after dark by the time the charter bus finally drove us through the ranch gate. There was no moon, but the stars dusted the entire valley with a faint glow. I more sensed than saw the dark mountain faces looming up behind the ranch.

By the time I finally climbed into my upper bunk I was too excited to sleep, even though I'd barely slept in the past two days. My mind kept spinning around only one thought: the next morning I would be paired with my new horse! I felt I would explode with the thrill of it all. Finally I drifted off to sleep, wrapped in the closeness of my dream.

CHAPTER 3

My Horse! My Horse!

We meet

The camp bell woke us at 7 a.m. We had no problems getting out of bed. This was a big day. As we headed to the dining hall I was startled to see the mountains' surfaces not covered by trees or other vegetation were light colored rock that gleamed almost white in the blazing sunlight, a stark contrast to their dark presence the night before.

These were my first mountains and I was struck by their magnificence, their jagged peaks soaring far higher than I had ever seen any land reach. At age 13 I normally wasn't turned on by scenery but the mountains took my breath away. For the three summers I was there, I never took their beauty and grandeur for granted.

As soon as we were released from breakfast, we raced down to the corrals where we first-timers were to meet the horse that would be ours until we went home. The girls who had been there the summer before would be reunited with their horses. Old hands at the ranch, they quickly scrambled to the top-most rails of the large corral to excitedly scan the swirl of more than 70 horses for a glimpse of their special horse.

The rest of us also climbed the sides of the corral, but as I did I felt as stiff as my new Levi's and Western boots. I could barely breathe. So much was riding on the next few minutes. I was filled with only one thought: which horse would be mine? Here at the ranch each girl's relationship with her horse was an exclusive one, like a marriage—to care for and, as I soon came to realize, to learn from while riding together through some of the wildest adventures of our young lives. This was big stuff.

In the blur of horses moving below me, there was only one that had caught my eye—a prancing black mare with a plume of a tail that arched beautifully. I loved black horses. She was the only one I saw in the corral—and she was flashy. I ached for a horse like that. My heart sank when I learned she was promised to a girl from the previous summer.

Sam was busy in the corral catching and bridling horses. One by one he called girls over to the corral gate to be reunited with her old friend from the summer before or be introduced to her new horse. I started to get nervous. What would I do if I got an old plug? It was too terrible to think about—but I did.

It was an agonizing wait, but fortunately not a long one. Finally Sam called to me and gestured to meet him at the corral gate. As I climbed to the ground, I couldn't see through the milling herd which horse he had in tow. When he put the reins in my hands for me to lead my new horse out of the corral I got my first full look at him. I started to cry; I was so disappointed.

"His name is Topper," Sam told me ignoring my tears. "He's a good horse. You two will do well together."

I couldn't see how either of those statements could possibly be true, thinking Sam didn't have a particularly high opinion of either me or my abilities with horses. I learned later that was not true, but in that moment I felt everything was wrong. My dream was smashed.

Topper outwardly exhibited neither flash nor energy. In fact, as I looked him over I thought, unkindly, I was interrupting his nap. His name said it all to me: no originality, just a knock off of the horse of a fading western star older than my father. He didn't seem like a horse I could ride the wind on. But there we were, thrown together.

Blinking back my tears, I reluctantly led Topper out of the corral. In those moments I saw nothing in him that hinted of the amazing adventures—fun, dangerous, and transcendent—we would share. I hadn't learned yet to see who he truly was. Nor did I catch even a glimpse of the surprising turns he and I would take toward, away and back to each other over those three summers, or the length and strength of the bond that has held him to me to this day.

However, as we moved through the gate I realized I held the lead to my horse—*my horse*—and in spite of myself I started to see him in a new light. My disappointment faded with each step we took to the hitching rail I tied him to where I groomed him until he shined. This took some doing since he had recently rolled in mud, something I was to discover he had a fondness for doing. I was already falling in love. I couldn't stop myself and didn't even want to try. After all, I was a horse crazy kid and this was my horse for the entire summer.

In my experiences with horses to date I'd learned how to groom, saddle, bridle and ride them, but I didn't really know them, a knowledge that comes from just hanging out with them day after day. None had been mine until now. And he—my new horse—was about to give me an education that would last a lifetime.

Getting to know him

I may have initially given the impression Topper was unfortunate looking. He wasn't. He just wasn't stunning. He was a little taller than average, was on the muscular, stocky side but not fat. He had a smooth back with the right amount of natural "saddle" and a nicely shaped rump. Three quarters of his mane fell beautifully to the left side of his neck, while the remainder fell stubbornly to the right. At first it bugged me. I even tried weighting the renegade portion so it fell to the left. However as soon as the weights were removed—sproing! Just like a gymnast it did a smooth back walkover to the side his genetics had placed it. I finally just accepted it.

Topper had wonderful eyes. They were calm and showed an intelligence and depth I totally missed at our introduction. I loved his ears. While they were a smidge on the large side, they weren't big rabbit ears sticking out every which way that can make a horse look deranged. I spent countless hours on his back, seeing our approaching destinations between those ears. I would learn a lot about how a horse talks with them, just one of many silent communication tools they use.

He had two small streaks of white on his face as if someone had lightly feathered him with the tip of a small brush. One was centered on his forehead and the other was slightly left of center lower on his face. Most of his body was a light caramel color. His mane, tail and legs were a darker reddish tone. His most distinctive marking was a dark red stripe down his back from mane to tail.

I asked the wranglers, Ben and Rocky, what color Topper was and about his stripe which I hadn't ever seen on a horse. Every time we girls asked them something we had to suffer more than a few minutes of teasing before we got our answer.

"That stripe's an eave spout for sweat," Ben said deadpan.

I was surprised they didn't agree on what Topper's color actually was, but they both nixed the "faded sorrel" category as I'd classified him. Rocky claimed he was a buckskin; Ben said he was a dun. Both choices sounded dull to me but I found buckskin slightly preferable. At least Dale Evan's horse, Buttermilk, was a buckskin. Who ever heard of a cowboy hero and his big beautiful dun? It turned out Ben was right. Topper was a red dun. I later learned that all duns, regardless of their color, have stripes down their backs.

His dun color was a common characteristic of the two breeds those at the ranch who knew about such things agreed made up his breed heritage—a mixture of Quarter Horse and Mustang. This was further underscored by his calm disposition (Quarter Horse) and his independence and intelligence (Mustang).

Finding our wavelength

It felt natural to talk to Topper and frequently he cocked one ear and sometimes both back in my direction. He often turned his head to look at me. As we became better acquainted and I began to learn his language, I realized he did like my talking to him. He'd close his eyes and lower his head saying, "I'm relaxed" in horse language. It also became natural for me to share quiet with him during the many hours we spent together each day. Sometimes after a long ride into the mountains I'd dismount and lean against his shoulder stroking his neck, other times just holding the flat of my hand on his big warm body as I looked out over the meadows and valleys below me.

Over time I progressively tested him by mounting and dismounting from both sides, combing his tail, walking around his hindquarters, handling his legs and feet, and climbing all over him bareback working up to sliding off over his tail when I was confident it would be fine with him. I wanted him to get used to my handling him and to trust me.

He was about as calm and tolerant a horse as you would ever want to meet—within limits. He had his unique system of boundary maintenance and justice complete with warning signals. When I crossed those lines, he had his creative ways of teaching me the error of my ways, and those lessons would be part of our adventures together.

I loved just hanging around him and the other horses because I have always found everything about them marvelous. Even their manure is Chanel No. 5 to me. Their smooth, sculpted bodies and exquisitely chiseled legs are gorgeous from any angle with the possible exception of looking up at their bellies and lower lips from underneath. That's not the most flattering view but it is an intimate one, lying in the grass with nothing more important to do than watch the clouds and your big friend grazing near you who could choose to wander off but stays close instead.

I never tried to train Topper to come when I called or perform any tricks or stunts. In the ranch environment such things seemed meaningless to me. He wasn't a trick pony or pet. He was my companion and my partner on the many journeys we took together.

He was also my radar. His senses were far more attuned to safe passage on the trail than mine. His instinctive consciousness focused on the immediate "what" and "where" of a situation. He wasn't distracted by conversations with friends, as I often was. I learned to pay attention to any changes in the tension in his body, any tightening of his muscles, the forward prick of his ears, his "danger alert" signals when he suddenly raised his head high or made snorting or snuffling sounds. What was he seeing, hearing, sensing? It took me a while to recognize his "study mode" in which he lowered his head with ears pricked forward remaining perfectly still, followed by scanning movements of his head and neck like a radar device.

Many times whatever had registered on his senses eventually came into my sensor range. Other times I never knew what it was that tripped his alarm system, but I could tell when his assessed threat level was back to normal. I quickly came to rely on his judgment.

I was learning that in a close, extended relationship with a horse something starts to flow between the two of you, not at a level of cognition but of two beings finding their way to each other on a common plane. I had always loved being around horses, but now I was discovering the connection of being with my horse. I began to experience the remarkable intimacy of hanging out with an animal that to the uninitiated largely seems to ignore you, of learning some of his language and getting on the same wavelength, seeing him as more than just a horse to ride.

With him I began to recognize the best relationships are those in which the two parties, even if they're different species, become more than they were when they met and that somehow the connection between the two feeds their growth even if it isn't entirely conscious. It isn't anything you plan. It just happens.

We seemed to encourage in each other the development of a certain amount of individuation. Sam recognized it. He told me about half way through my stay at the ranch that he'd always liked Topper and found him a good solid horse. However, he told me, it wasn't until Topper became my horse that many of his talents and distinctive personality traits started coming out—and, likewise, that I appeared to flourish with him.

It took me decades to acknowledge Topper was always a grownup in our relationship, a role I could not always claim. I loved him and I had some hard lessons in what that meant. He had his ways of demonstrating he liked me in his life, but it wasn't until my last summer at the ranch that I had concrete evidence, in horse dynamics, that he loved me and was glad I was in his life. But I'm way ahead of myself.

CHAPTER 4

Topper Earns a New Name

Our introduction to barrel racing

One of Topper's eccentricities was revealed early in our first summer together when he and I were introduced to barrel racing. This was rodeo country and barrel racing was the only sport open to women in the rodeo arena. So several of us decided we were going to learn.

The "barrels," as it is often called, is a timed race run in a cloverleaf pattern. Three large barrels, oil drums actually, are set up very much like a baseball diamond. Horse and rider start from a place equivalent to home plate and race toward the first-base barrel, making a fast, sharp and clean turn around it. Next they streak across what would be the pitcher's mound to the third-base barrel, moving tightly and quickly around it before racing to the third and last barrel in the second-base position. Once that barrel is rounded, horse and rider run to home-plate position. Anyway, that's the way it's supposed to be.

Barrel racing is a partnership between horse and rider. Both need to enjoy it to be good at it. I thought it would be great fun. At the time I had no concept of a horse having any preference in the matter. My friend Sandy, her mare Molly, and Topper and I waited in line for our turns. Sandy said she noticed that both our horses watched the other horses as they took their runs, but most of the other horses didn't. She said Molly was good at the barrels, so maybe the fact that Topper watched meant he was interested. He wasn't, we soon learned—not the least bit. But he didn't let on until it was our turn.

What fresh hell is this?

I'd like to say in his defense that he was a good horse as Sam had first told me. He had wonderful gaits, he was calm, he responded well and immediately to all commands—at least to date. He was the least spooky of any horse I've ever known. He did things for me I sensed weren't on top of his list of things he liked to do, like jumping fallen logs, irrigation ditches and stony mountain creeks. Still, he did them well. So when it was our turn for the barrels I assumed he'd do what I asked.

Either my sensors weren't working that day or he kept all signals inside. We pounded toward the first barrel just as I'd seen the others do. It felt good. I aimed him to start the turn at what I judged to be the right point to make a tight arc around the barrel. But when I reined him into the turn, he slammed on the brakes so suddenly I almost went off because I was already leaning into the turn. He then walked around the barrel. Actually, it was more of a stroll, the spectators gleefully reported later.

I was a little in shock and hoped he was just feeling his way. I knew I sure was. We raced over to the second barrel only to have him do his little cakewalk around it, too. I heard Sandy call out, "Shift that tank out of first gear." When I pointed him to the third barrel, he again sprang into action. And as we approached the turn I kicked him with my heels several times and slapped his neck with the ends of the reins. However, he took No. 3 the way he had the first two, but he was willing to make the final run for home fast. Everyone was laughing.

I was a decent rider but by no means the most experienced rider at the ranch. Sandy held that distinction. I asked her if she'd take him around in case the problem was my inexperience. She agreed and off they went, only to see him repeat his performance.

As she handed his reins back to me she laughed and said, "He'll only do those barrel turns like a tank."

The name stuck. He was from that point forever and always, Tank.

I don't know if he thought barrels were beneath him or what. He'd never seemed particular or even stubborn about things before but after these two performances we all agreed he had nothing but disdain for barrel racing. I'm sure a good trainer could have gotten him to take those barrel turns with some speed, but he made a stand and I had to admire the calculated showmanship with which he did it. Normally I would have insisted on my way—him being a horse and my being a rider who's supposed to be in charge—but for some reason I let it slide with him and the barrels. He did what I needed a western saddle-horse to do, so I left the barrels alone and cheered on the others.

CHAPTER 5

Life on the Ranch

Sam and Betty

Sam and his wife, Betty, ran the ranch. All of us girls had met Sam when he came to our homes in the winter, but we didn't meet Betty until we got to the ranch. Together they oversaw all ranch operations and us. Sam was in charge of anything to do with horses, other livestock, and all things outside. Betty was the camp nurse and cook. We all liked Sam, but Betty—not so much.

She had the look of a once beautiful woman who had dried and hardened in the harsh elements of ranch life. Her hands and voice were both over-sized and rough. It was impossible to predict how an encounter with her would go. I never knew whether she'd be nice or snarl a nasty comment. When I had to interact with her I did so cautiously, minimizing our contact as much as possible.

Sam was the one with whom we had the most contact. He was good about giving us long leashes, but before he let us out on them he made sure we knew the rules—about safety of the horses and us. His voice and demeanor commanded authority and we respected that. While he was a lot of fun and wanted us to have fun too, he also had a temper. Normally, he was pretty good at keeping it in check but you could tell when you'd tripped one of his wires. He got instantly quiet and his face flamed deep red under his tan. He rarely erupted, though, keeping himself in check.

However, there was one big exception—shoeing horses. It brought out the worst in Sam.

Horses have to get new shoes an average of every six to eight weeks. How fast they wear down depends on several variables, including the types of terrain they travel, how they move their feet, and the condition of their hooves.

From a technical standpoint Sam was a good horse-shoer. He cleaned, clipped and filed the hooves expertly. He sized and shaped the shoes well and nailed them on straight. However, he had no patience with horses that were touchy or fearful about being shod. Unfortunately he often treated this behavior as rebellion rather than fear. Any skittish movements could send Sam completely off the rails. He'd do things like grab the offending (frightened) horse's lead rope and repeatedly jerk it hard while yelling at top volume, or kick the horse in the ribs or gut or smack it with a shovel. Or he'd pepper the poor animal with whatever was handy—metal hoof rasps or horseshoes. There was no carry-over equity. If a horse had previously been good during shoeing but at the next shoeing acted out, it caught the wrath of Sam. It wasn't pretty. In fact, it was pretty scary.

At that age and in that decade, we kids weren't good about defending ourselves from out-of-line behavior by adults. I didn't like to be around when shoeing was happening because Sam's explosive anger at frightened animals to me was inexcusable. But we needed to be there when our horses were shod, to stand at their heads, talk soothingly and hold their lead ropes. I was grateful that Tank took shoeing as calmly as he took most other things.

Still, Sam was the architect of our ranch experiences. A former teacher, he taught us, he encouraged us, he played with us, and led many of our adventures. I learned more about horses from Sam than any other person. In most situations he maintained his cool and could be incredibly patient.

The ranch setting

The ranch nestled up against mountains that framed the edges of a long valley. The elevation of the valley floor ranged from 6,500 to 7,500 feet—and that was just our starting point. Adjusting to the altitude was a rough process at the beginning of each summer. For two to three days many of us experienced, in varying degrees, headaches, dizziness, and nausea. Unless symptoms were severe, we just kept going. No one wanted to miss out on anything, particularly at the front end of this great adventure. Besides, I quickly proved you could barf just as easily from the back of a horse as you could anywhere else. The most important and considerate thing was to first check wind direction.

We slept in cabins that held up to 12 girls each. A counselor was assigned to each cabin, usually someone college age who had been a camper at the ranch. Cabins were furnished with creaky bunk beds and each girl had a few drawers in one of several dressers either grouped in the middle of the room or stuffed between the beds. Our trunks were shoved under the beds and used as extra storage space.

Each cabin had a covered front porch with about three steps leading up to it. There were no porch railings or chairs. I loved the bootjacks in the edges of the porches. Bootjacks are half circles cut into the ends of planks where you insert the heel of your boot to pull your foot out. It's a lot easier than sitting with your foot in your lap wrestling like a contortionist to get your boots off.

This was a no frills camp. There was electricity, but no plumbing in the cabins. There were outhouses—"three and four holers" as we called them—a respectable distance behind the cabins on the other side of the creek that ran behind the cabins and down through the corrals. There was a central bathhouse with flush toilets and showers up by the dining hall and meeting lodge, but the outhouses got the most use.

Recreation & entertainment

There were no tennis courts, swimming pools or archery ranges. Our focus was on the horses, ranch operations and exploring the wild mountainous areas that ringed our world. Our days were filled with being with our horses. But we did have free time some evenings after the horses were turned loose for the night to graze in the open range of the foothills immediately behind the ranch. We did what kids living on ranches and farms all over the world did—we found ways to entertain ourselves using our imaginations and group games that could be played with little or no equipment.

Regardless of how the game started and what its intended finish was to be, it generally morphed into some form of chase, catch and tickle whoever you could get on the ground. This often resulted in a pile of giggling squealing girls. Occasionally Sam joined us. He'd toss a bucket of water on us or take handfuls of ice he'd brought from the kitchen to drop down the backs of our shirts. Then we'd all chase him! You would have thought we were a boys' camp at times. One evening I was brought down by a flying tackle from the rear and injured my knee. For several days I couldn't walk without great difficulty, but once I was in the saddle I was good to go.

Another favorite evening pastime was to ride Big Ed, a Percheron, the largest breed of horse. True to his breed he was a gentle giant with a marvelously calm disposition. He also was so tall that the only way we could mount him was from the top rails of one of the corrals. We could get about five girls on his back without causing him distress. Some Percherons are lean and graceful looking while others, like Big Ed, are quite stocky (both acceptable variations of the breed). Ed was a bulky boy, so much so that once we were seated on top of him—always bareback—our legs stuck out awkwardly on either side of his great broad back.

To say one "rode" Big Ed is misleading, implying whoever held his reins steered his movements. What actually steered Big Ed was true love. Utterly devoted to a mare named Sugar, he went where she went, his nose right on her tail. Big Ed's quest for Sugar could not be thwarted—not by his riders or the unalterable fact that he was a gelding (neutered male), rendered unable to consummate any relationship.

Then in the spring before my second summer Sugar had a filly that looked exactly like her, if you were looking through the wrong end of a telescope. We named her Sweetie. So when Sam bought a Welsh Pony the same color as Big Ed (which he claimed was pure coincidence) and half his size, there was only one name we could give him—Little Ed, which eventually morphed into Eddie. Furthermore, Eddie adored Big Ed, and only Big Ed, following him everywhere.

I had to laugh every time I saw the four of them, and when they were on their own time it was *always* the four of them. Sugar led the procession followed by her miniaturized double, followed immediately by Big Ed, trailed by his tiny twin, Eddie.

But my favorite among favorites of evening activities was something we only got to do a couple of times each summer. About eight miles from the ranch was a small town which boasted of a post office, a couple of stores, a gas station, a few scattered homes, and most important—rodeo grounds where a rodeo was held every Saturday night. We rode our horses there, starting out in the late afternoon. We took a pack lunch for dinner wrapped in a jacket or poncho tied to the back of the saddle, along with a requisite winter jacket in case it was cold when we returned later that night.

It wasn't a fancy rodeo or even a good rodeo by any standards. But we loved it because it was all local talent, including the horses and cattle provided by local ranchers and other residents for the bucking broncs, calf roping, steer riding and bulldogging events. During the rest of the week some of these animals, but not all, were saddle horses or cattle being raised for beef. When a bucking cinch (used by all rodeos) was tightened around them in front of their hind legs—a very sensitive area—they could often put on a decent enough performance as bucking broncs or steers.

We returned to the ranch on the back road at the base of the foothills—unpaved and no cars. The only hints of civilization we saw were occasional lights from ranch houses in the distance. It was often cold, so cold that our horses blew out cloudy breaths as we huddled down in our warm jackets. I loved to listen to the creak of Tank's saddle under me, and to his occasional huffing and snorting as packs of coyotes ramped up their yipping to eerie, howling crescendos that made me glad I had a cabin and warm bed to go to, but sad I had to leave such a primal serenade to do so.

Friendships at the ranch

Most of our activities and adventures were with the girls we shared a cabin with except when we were all out of camp on pack trips, rough rides or some other trip. Consequently, our friendships were largely formed with our cabin mates. There is something about the closeness of living, sleeping, eating and playing together that contributes to forming tight friendships—the center piece of the camping experience. There's a verse from a poem about camp friends I picked up somewhere along the way that I feel says it best:

> You've shared so much in sun and rain,
> Foolish things and wise;
> And 'neath the candid gaze of stars
> Have worn no cheap disguise.

The camp had two sessions each summer: one for five weeks and one for six weeks. Most of the girls only came for one session, including counselors. Sandy, Shannon and I were among those who stayed for both sessions. We became close friends, supported by the extended time we spent together over the course of both sessions each summer, nearly always in the same cabin.

The strongest bonding factor for our friendship, no doubt, was that we each craved the rough, primitive life with horses we shared in the last vestiges of the Old West. We couldn't get enough of it, unlike the vast majority of our cabin mates who clearly did—needing breaks from the dirt, the elements and the physical exertion we expended daily.

I had spent the previous five summers at a camp with a much tamer environment to which a majority of campers returned year after year. This, I was surprised to learn, was not the case at the ranch. A much smaller percentage of girls returned for another summer or two. Among those were two girls who also became good friends, Katie and Pam. They both came all three summers I was there, but only for one session.

Katie, Shannon and I loved seeing how far we could go in certain situations, just how much we could get away with. Our antics entertained Sandy but she often preferred being a part of the audience rather than an active participant. So did Pam, but we usually managed to recruit her anyway as a reluctant accomplice in our adventures.

The ranch provided an additional friendship category and the most important for many of us—our horses. We shared as much time and space together with them as with each other, sometimes more. I feel I got to know Tank more intimately than many of the girls I shared a cabin with.

Ranch attire & outfitting

Unlike most other private camps there were no uniforms. Well, there were but you couldn't order them from the Marshall Field's camping department. We wore Levi's—boys' Levi's. If a girl came with any other brand she would be subject to teasing about her "dude" jeans and would often plead with her parents to send her Levi's, or to arrange with Sam for her to buy them in town.

However, as kids we all knew what we were up against with parents, so if the situation wasn't resolvable—as in the case of one girl's grandmother insisting on her wearing side zipper girl's jeans (what proper ladies wore)—we understood.

Also included in our ranch wardrobe were cotton shirts of our choosing, sweatshirts, a Levi jacket, and western boots commonly called cowboy boots. I rarely remember us wearing anything else. For really dress occasions, like going to a big rodeo miles away or riding our horses in small-town parades as we did sometimes, we wore freshly washed jeans and a clean rodeo shirt.

Rodeo shirts were new to me. I fell in love with them. They have fancy buttons or snaps with metal or pearly looking covers. Many of them are made from richer fabrics and colors than standard shirts and have colored piping across the chest and back, down the sleeves and around the cuffs. My first summer, my aunt gave me a beautiful cream-colored shirt with gorgeous red piping. The first time I wore it was for a small town Fourth of July rodeo parade we rode in. Actually, we were the entire parade.

We waited in a large field just off the main street for the parade organizers to tell us when it was time to line up. We had dismounted and held our horses' reins as we let them graze the tall, lush grass. There were lots of flies and everyone swatted at them. Suddenly Tank's head shot up which he rapidly rubbed up and down my front to get rid of the flies attacking his face, leaving big green streaks of horse slobber all over the front of my lovely new shirt. After that I preferred dark colors like red or black.

We lived in our boots. We rode in them, walked in them, climbed steep rocky mountain trails in them, and splashed through creeks in them. They took a terrific beating and we didn't really take care of them as well as we should have. One pair of good quality, leather western boots only lasted me one season. Each summer I went off to the ranch with a new pair of boots.

When we packed out for several days to some remote part of the valley or high up in the mountains, we took few extra clothes because there wasn't room to haul much except essentials. Standard contents of our duffels included: one sleeping bag with a heavy wool blanket folded into it for the cold nights, a change of underwear for every day, not quite so many changes of socks, a couple of extra shirts, an extra pair of Levi's, a sweatshirt, and a winter jacket. Tied on the backs of our saddles, if we weren't already wearing them, were the standard issue rain poncho and, of course, a Levi jacket.

We never slept in tents. We slept out under the stars, our sleeping bags lined up toe-to-toe in two rows of 10 to 12 girls. Our protection against rain, snow, and the cold was a large heavy tarp for each line of sleeping bags. During good weather it was rolled up at our feet. When we needed cover we pulled it up over our heads like a big blanket. I've never had a tent as efficient at keeping out the elements as those tarps. Unless it rained or snowed I lay looking up at the stars so much brighter and several thousand feet closer than they were at home. To this day no matter where I am on the planet, when I look up at the stars I often think of those nights, how bright and beckoning the lights of the heavens were.

It wasn't unusual to wake up in the morning covered with frost or a light dusting of snow. Normally not much of a morning person, out on pack trips I looked forward to being awakened by the sun and lay peeking out from under the tarp to watch the steadily advancing line of sunlight melt the sparkling icy ground cover as it moved.

Painful riding lesson

I'd never ridden bareback before coming to the ranch. I wasn't the only one. This blank spot in my riding résumé was quickly filled in under Sam's "learn-by-doing" tutelage. We were going to a big rodeo quite a distance away where we would camp out for a couple of days. This meant the horses had to be ridden to a large pasture seven miles from the ranch and we were going to have to ride them there. Sam would pick us up in the open top cattle truck we traveled in for any trip on wheels. Our duffels were already stacked in the back where we used them as makeshift cushions, leaving no room for saddles, only for bridles which would have to make the trip with us.

"I want you all to ride bareback to the pasture and we can head out from there," he told us. "You're going to have to ride at a fast trot because we're running late."

My heart froze—seven miles at a fast trot, the hardest gait to learn to sit bareback. In fact, it's brutal if you're a rank bareback beginner. I don't know which of us was more uncomfortable, Tank or me, as I bounced awkwardly and sometimes wildly around on his back clinging desperately to his mane and occasionally his neck. He wore what I came to recognize as his "I'm not happy" ears, held at a funny angle out to the side and back, twitching most of the ride. Well, I wasn't happy either but I didn't fall off once. I felt like kissing the ground when we got to the pasture.

I soon grew to love riding bareback—not that day I'll tell you—and got good at it as well as getting up on Tank's back which could be challenging since he was not a small horse. My favorite bareback mounting method was pure TV cowboy inspired by countless hours of after-school viewing. I'd stand at his shoulder facing his rump, grab his reins and a handful of mane and swing my right leg up and over his back to land sitting upright. That's how it's supposed to happen. If I didn't get my leg at least three-quarters of the way across his spine, I inelegantly clung to his side, like a crab crawling up a seawall, for a split second before sliding earthward. It worked best when he was slightly downhill from me.

Another method, utterly lacking in grace, was to jump up so I sprawled on my stomach across his back, head hanging over his other side. The briefer the time spent in this position the better. I'd then inch and kick my way forward to get my right leg over his back without punching him too much with my knees or elbows to eventually arrive at a sitting position.

Mostly Tank stood patiently when my efforts to mount him bareback involved struggle, which I'm proud to say happened less and less over those three summers. However, if I took too long (I was never clear on just what his measurement of that was) or dug my knees or elbows into him one too many times (another measurement on a sliding scale), and always when I was precariously balanced, he'd walk briskly (the only way

I could be sure I'd overstepped one of his boundaries), turning in a tight circle always in the direction providing the best chance of my falling off. When this happened he'd immediately stop, then turn to look at me as if saying, "What are you doing down there?"

Learning to be ranch hands

Although there were always at least one or two professional wranglers, we girls were the day-to-day ranch hands. We loaded hay, groomed horses, shoveled out the cow barn, cleaned and polished our tack, and did whatever tasks we were asked. It didn't seem like work to me.

My second summer one of the ranch dairy cows developed mastitis, a painful infection of the udder. I was given the assignment to care for her. Because of her condition she needed to be hand milked and her milk discarded. I also had to soak her udder before each milking. I found it ironic that I lived in Wisconsin, the nation's dairy state, and had to go all the way to the Rocky Mountains to learn how to milk a cow. Sam supervised me at first until we both were confident I could do it. Once I got past my fingers cramping I got fairly good at milking.

Learning to milk a cow is like learning to diaper a baby boy. You have to know how to protect yourself from getting hit in the face. It's their tails. They're not like horse tails. The bottom portion is brush-like, comprised of many long hairs. When you're sitting on a stool up close and personal to a cow's hindquarters that tail can deliver a surprising wallop when it hits you in the face. I learned to split the tail hairs into two parts and tie them around the cow's hind leg. I only forgot once to untie her tail when I finished milking. I didn't notice it until I turned her back into the pasture and saw her captive loop of a tail jerking back and forth as she walked. I ran out into the pasture and quickly untied it. Cows are some of the sweetest creatures on earth.

During those three summers I came to detest fresh milk. While our cows produced enough milk for everyone to drink in a day and even though it was refrigerated, it didn't have enough time to get cold the way I like it. Although the milk was pasteurized it was not homogenized. That meant there were all these floating yellow fat globules that clung unappetizingly to the sides of the glass. Plus it tasted like whatever the cows had been eating—mountain flowers, wild onions and, of course, the sagebrush that carpeted much of the valley floor. Its distinct pungent odor permeated everything. Even our canteens tasted of sage, a seasoning I use sparingly to this day as a result.

Chapter 6

On the Trail

Wrangling, the choicest job

Wrangling consists of driving a herd of horses from one point to another. Sam was selective about which girls were chosen for this work. Since the wrangling we did was largely unsupervised, he needed to know we had a proven record of being responsible, attentive and good at handling the often unpredictable behavior of horses.

There wasn't a large pool of girls for him to tap for wrangling. While all the girls at the ranch loved horses, most stopped short of the total immersion Sandy, Shannon and I craved. Many thought wrangling was drudgery—a lot of "eating dust" at an often plodding pace. Consequently, we three performed a lot of the wrangling duties at the ranch. And that was just fine with us.

Sandy was the top wrangler among the girls. She didn't just have experience with horses, she was gifted in the expert way she handled them. Also she had spent more summers at the ranch than any of us, starting when she was much younger. Shannon was next in line in horse and wrangling skills. By my second summer I was becoming a good, overall wrangler, largely thanks to the two of them.

Wrangling enabled us to live and breathe horses all day and into the night, even round-the-clock when we were out on a pack trip. Being with horses is about being in the elements because the out-of-doors is their environment: the dirt, the wind, flies, ticks, mosquitoes, rain, snow and hail—and there we were with them. It wasn't easy and it certainly wasn't a life of comfort. We just accepted it.

Every day we were prepared for these possibilities, for high up in the mountains weather could and did change rapidly and unexpectedly. Even with our gear to protect us if it was really cold we eventually got cold. If it rained steadily we got wet. During those times I sometimes leaned way over Tank's neck as I rode and wrapped my arms around him, pressing against the warmth of his big body.

It was as close to God as I could get.

Wrangling—the reality

Additional wrangling duties consisted of driving the horses more than 30 miles to the site of our base camp when we packed out. Occasionally we all rode our horses there but most girls usually chose to go by truck with the duffels, especially if it was raining. My choice was always to go by horse. Any opportunity to be with my horse or ride my horse, especially to wrangle, I took. And I wasn't particular about the weather.

Wrangling horses all day long is slow, dirty work. Unlike in the movies you don't wrangle at a gallop. No one can run 30 miles. You go most of the way at a steady walk. Sometimes it was boring, but not often since I was on my horse with many other horses in a place of horses. There was a rhythm you got caught up in: the bobbing of 70 horses' heads, the swishing of 70 tails, the flicking of 70 pairs of ears, the soft thudding beat of hooves in the powdery dirt. To this day, I have never found an environment in which I feel more at home.

These were the same rhythms of the many western songs we sang together as we rode. I came to recognize their origins through experiences we shared with those who composed them more than a century before.

When wrangling horses you usually trail rather than lead, so our hair and clothing became coated with a noticeable dusting of trail dirt, our faces often caked with it. Even so when we saw tourists' cars up ahead or heard them coming from behind, we dug down in our Levi jacket pockets for the half-melted tubes of lipstick we all kept stashed for such occasions. There might be boys in those cars!

I have never been so dirty for such extended periods as I was my three summers at the ranch. We often packed out for several days at a time and went that long without bathing—something that would have driven us all nuts in any other situation, but there it just felt natural, to me anyway, and most accepted it. Even if you wanted to bathe, many creeks were only a few inches deep, enough for tooth brushing, face washing, and some sponge bathing but not much else. The deeper creeks had snow melt as their water source. Stepping into them reminded me of the time I fell through the ice one winter in Wisconsin. Only those truly desperate to wash—most of us at least once—stripped and dipped in those creeks.

When we got back to the ranch we stood in the showers and watched the dirt we'd hosted for days roll across the shower floor to the drain and wondered how we could have ferried that much grit. Clearly these were not the things we wrote home about.

Night rider duty—advanced wrangling

Wrangling horses to a specific destination is relatively easy. The challenging part is to keep them in a contained area, without the aid of fences, once you get there. Since our pack trips took us many miles from the ranch it was crucial that we kept our horses with us. It would be a long walk back without them. My first time out as a night rider I had the 2- 4 a.m. shift. I really got schooled that night. The other two girls and I on this shift were hyper-vigilant about keeping the herd together. We felt equipped for the task. We weren't.

We herded them too tightly and didn't recognize the warning signs. When they got restless we closed in—a big mistake. The best thing to do, we learned too late, is to back off and give them more room and sometimes they'll settle down. When they started to move in a circular pattern, rapidly gaining speed, that was it. We had lost control. They bolted and all we could do was helplessly watch them leave.

I'd thought I was experienced enough to keep them contained. Yet here I was feeling as inept as any tenderfoot. I got to hear Sam echo those same opinions of my performance at pretty high volume when I had to wake him at 3:30 to tell him the horses were gone. It was not pleasant. We spent the next day retrieving horses from all over the mountain. However, I was forgiven and better prepared for the next time.

Well, you have to have a little fun

Sandy, Shannon and I were regularly given the responsibility of wrangling the horses out to the highway a few evenings a week to graze the volunteer hay that grew on the wide strips of land on either side of the not well-traveled, mostly unpaved, two lane highway running by the ranch. Some of the fields closest to the ranch grew hay and over the years the seeds drifted out of those fields to produce a highway beltline of hay, a higher quality grazing than was available in the foothills behind the ranch where our horses did the majority of their grazing.

Evening road duty normally took a couple of hours and it wasn't all work. I must confess we occasionally took some liberties to amuse ourselves—like the evening Shannon decided to ride Suzy Q, a retired Quarter Horse racer Sam had just bought. She had been itching to ride her, but Sam wasn't letting anyone on her yet. Shannon said she felt certain no one at the ranch would see if she just hopped on for a little trial spin. While we were visible from the ranch we were too far away for anyone to see what we were actually doing unless high-powered binoculars were used.

We always took a halter and long lead rope with us, just in case we needed them. This was the only time I remember they were ever used. Shannon grabbed the halter and walked down to Suzy Q who was on the far side of the herd. She put the halter on her and fashioned the lead rope through it to serve as reins. A bridle with a curb bit might have prevented what happened next—though maybe not.

Once Shannon hopped on her back and urged her forward, true to her breed and training, Suzy Q ramped up and was flat out in seconds. Until that moment I had never seen a horse go that fast so quickly—and to see it so close up! We also saw that Shannon's efforts to control her had no effect. I learned that night retired racers still strived to be out in front of the pack. As the two of them sped by us like a Roadrunner cartoon, spewing gravel and clouds of dust, Shannon called out, "I can't stop her!" That, we told her later, qualified for understatement of the year!

Sandy said if we chased her on our horses it would only encourage Suzy Q, so we stood there and helplessly watched, pointlessly calling out to Shannon to hang on. After Suzy Q passed all the other horses, whose only movements were chewing and swallowing, certain of her victory she slowed down. Shannon slid off her back and shakily leaned against her for a few minutes before starting back—on foot.

I had never had a horse run away with me. It was a good lesson: know a lot about the horse you jump on to ride with just a halter.

Later we asked Sam if Suzy Q had a good racing record.

"Oh, yes," he told us smiling, making us think he might have had some binoculars out…

And then there was the problem of Sergeant—a bony, old gelding kept around for the occasional girl who knew nothing about horses.

Sergeant was docile and otherwise unremarkable except for one quirk. He hated moving cars. No one knew why because when he came to the ranch he was well beyond his colt years. If a car was in striking distance and moved under 25 miles per hour, there was a high probability of him bashing it. Normally not the fastest thing on hooves, he could move like lightening, whirling and kicking (with or without a rider) as the offending vehicle drove by which unfortunately for the driver was usually quite slowly. The adage "no good deed goes unpunished" springs to mind for those considerate people who slowed down when they saw they were sharing the road with a herd of horses.

We had to be on the lookout for cars and drive Sergeant away from the edge of the road when any approached. Occasionally—OK, I admit it—we didn't try very hard. Sergeant's victims usually just stood there surveying the damage not really knowing what to say. Mostly they wound up laughing and told us it would make a great story when they got back home. Only rarely did an angry Sergeant casualty drive up to the ranch to have a chat with Sam. However, at that time in that part of the West, the horse was king.

We drew a lot of attention from tourists. Seeing girls on horseback driving a herd of horses was something they just didn't see in Illinois, Ohio or Indiana. They didn't know many of us were from those states, too. And we never let on that we were anything other than ranching girls at work with our horses. For during those summers, that's exactly what we were. Cars slowed down and even stopped, movie cameras whirring (there were no video recorders then). We'd often ham it up by driving the horses faster, completely unnecessary but the tourists didn't know that. Over the course of three years, Tank and I were in a lot of home movies.

Above the timberline—not so much fun

At least once a summer we packed out above the timberline, my least favorite place with its thin air and sparse, stunted vegetation. We girls normally talked back and forth to each other while riding, but on our way there we were quiet as our horses picked their way over narrow rocky trails hugging sheer cliffs and around tight hair-pin turns chiseled into the mountains' edges. When you made those turns all you could see between your horse's ears was empty space and a straight drop of hundreds of feet. You didn't want to look, but you couldn't help but look.

My life was literally in the hands of another species. I kept reminding myself Tank didn't want to go over the edge any more than I did. I trusted him and told him so as we rode. I think he was fine without my steady verbal reassurance, but it made me feel better. It comforted me to remember the timeline murals from science classes picturing the development of different life forms on earth indicating horses had survived on this planet for at least 50 million years. Humans came along considerably later with a much shorter record of survival. It also helped that my father, who had grown up with horses, told me when you're out in back country on horseback and you lose your way or aren't sure whether the passageway you're considering is safe or stable, let your horse have its head and trust its judgment.

And to complicate matters, everything had to be packed in on horseback. Horses not assigned to any girl were drafted into service as packhorses. Everyone had to lead one. You didn't want to fasten its lead rope securely to your saddle horn or anything else because if by some horrible chance a horse went over the edge it wouldn't take another with it. So all day long you held a thick lead rope to a packhorse that didn't necessarily like being a packhorse, and held it loosely enough to let the horse go if something happened, but tightly enough to stay connected. The lead rope sawed across your thigh, sometimes generating red welts by the end of the day.

A rough way of life

I came to empathize greatly with those who fought their way west on wagon trains and who, history records, only traveled a few miles each day because so much of the time was spent hitching teams, loading wagons, unloading them, feeding animals, setting up camp, hunting food and preparing it, and one other critical activity—surviving.

At the end of the summer it was a major adjustment to re-enter civilization. You couldn't just flip a switch. It helped to stay in touch with ranch friends. I only lived a couple of hours from Katie and Pam, and our parents were good about letting us go for visits over long weekends or a few days over Christmas or spring vacations. Sandy and Shannon lived farther away and we wrote letters to each other. However, our horses were still out West in some icy, snowy pasture. Each winter I had a calendar on which I marked off the weeks until finally I could be on the train heading back to the ranch.

CHAPTER 7

Playing TV Cowboy

Just had to try it

I occasionally had to demonstrate my inner daredevil by replicating some stunt I'd seen modeled by TV cowboys whose horses came when called, stood by obediently except when a run for help was needed, used their teeth to untie ropes to free the heroes, or did whatever was necessary not requiring opposable thumbs to rescue their human partners from their harrowing predicaments.

One such opportunity occurred early in my ranch experience when a few of us went "off lead"—no counselor or wrangler with us—to explore an area a couple of miles from our base camp on a pack trip. There we stumbled onto an abandoned corral. Judging by its appearance it was left over from a much earlier time. Its entrance was crowned with a high cross bar. In the movies, these were usually topped with a cow's skull. This one had no skull but it still inspired me. It had the added bonus that it appeared to be in easy reach to grab on to—if I were standing up in the saddle—and then swing up to sit on top of the bar. To be daring I would have to do this while Tank was traveling at a lope (slow gallop). Once I grabbed the bar the rest would be easy, or so I thought.

I'd developed a reputation for out-of-the-box behaviors, which is probably why no one tried to dissuade me. In fact, Katie and Pam egged me on. I did a few practice runs some distance from the corral gate, getting into a crouch on the saddle and finding ways to anchor my feet in the stirrup leathers high up under the fenders so I could get to the point where I could stand at the crucial moment. I also wanted Tank to get used to me moving around awkwardly on his back. I tied the ends of his reins together to rest on his neck so he wouldn't step on them when I departed his back.

When I felt ready, I headed him toward the corral at a lope. I knew I wouldn't have any trouble getting him through the gate at this speed because the corral was quite large. How I got or kept my footing for those few seconds I needed to stand and grab the bar is beyond me. I didn't feel that steady but somehow managed to time it so I stood just as we got to the gate. By some miracle it worked. After I left his back, Tank continued with stirrups flapping like wings, stopping when he reached the center of the corral.

No career as a stunt double in my future

I hadn't thought this through. For starters, there was no swinging up to the top of the bar. Instead I hung there like wet laundry. The cross bar I held onto was rough and cut into my hands, and while I was always quite athletic, I was never a gymnast. I called to Pam and Katie—who at that point found my predicament hilarious—and asked if one of them could please bring Tank back so I could jump onto his back.

Katie was no help, wheezing through her laughter she was going to pee in her pants. So Pam led Tank toward the gate where I uncomfortably hung. Faced with the reality that it was a lot farther going down to land in a seated position (ouch!) in the saddle than it was to grab the bar from a standing position, I now had serious second thoughts about dropping down on him.

Apparently, Tank shared my concern. As he approached the gate, I turned around in order for us to face the same direction so I missed seeing some of the rapidly unfolding events. Here's what happened according to reports of those present, supplemented by my brief observations: When Tank got just a few feet from me he suddenly pivoted on his hind legs, ripping his reins free from a very surprised Pam. He then wheeled again and made a dash through the gate into open territory. All I saw was him streaking to freedom to the left of my dangling legs.

I was relieved that fate—in the form of my Tank—had intervened. I then carefully maneuvered over to the edge of the cross bar, put my feet on solid corral rails and climbed down. Tank had run some distance away and once in his prescribed safety zone stopped and started grazing. His reins slid easily down his neck to allow this. He continued grazing as I walked up to him, collected his reins, rubbed his neck, scratched the base of his ears under his bridle, got on and rode off. We never spoke of it again.

But Katie did. That winter during one of our visits she showed me a copy of a theme she'd written for English class about the events of that day. Her teacher's note under the big red "A" read: "The detailed descriptions are wonderful—more themes on Debbie's antics, please!"

CHAPTER 8

Rough Rides

That wasn't in the brochure!

Sam was big on what he called rough rides up in the mountains high above the valley floor. Next to wrangling these rides were my favorite adventures at the ranch. This despite the fact I was nearly killed on two of them. It's a good thing they were only vaguely alluded to in the camp promotional materials as "scenic ridge rides" showing pictures of smiling, waving girls on horseback in some high mountain meadow, never depicting what perils those girls and their horses had to go through to get there. I'm sure if some parents knew what actually went on during those rides they wouldn't have let their precious little girls loose for such primitive and sometimes dangerous experiences. But I loved it.

We went on three or four rough rides each summer. There were no trails where we went. No matter what we encountered we found our way through or around it. We never reversed course—at least that was the plan. The rides were a balance of following the edges of the mountain ridges rimming our valley and exploring the high meadows and strange little valleys tucked in the steep slopes and deep folds of the mountains that looked as though a giant had punched them out with his fists.

I was always disappointed that my photos only captured fractions of the vast raw beauty of the landscapes we and our horses scrambled up and over. It was awesome to peer over the edge of a sheer drop all the way down to the valley floor only to turn moments later to find a broad expanse of meadows sweeping majestically upward to more ridges and icy mountain peaks beyond.

Learning why they're called rough rides

On my first rough ride I found out why they were so named. It was midmorning when we reached an incline so steep that the only way to get up and over it was to dismount, hold onto the reins of your horse, and grab the tail of the horse ahead of you to switchback up the slope. I was surprised at this, thinking that hauling up the mountain hanging onto their tails would make the horses edgy. Surprisingly it didn't. This may seem like an unusual mode of mountain travel, but it was one we used several times.

Tank and I were toward the end of the line. About 30 girls and their horses already snaked their way up in this manner. I was about to dismount to take my place in the line when someone up-hill from me screamed my name followed by, "LOOK OUT!" If I had turned toward the voice two seconds sooner, the rock bouncing right for me would have hit me in the face instead of the back of my head. I was knocked unconscious.

I was told later when I fell off Tank I fell out to one side, still holding his reins in my hand which yanked his head around, almost to his shoulder, pulling him off balance. When I came to I felt groggy and was nauseated from the sickening sweet, pungent odors of mountain flowers. Lying flat on the ground I saw I was surrounded by four, red trembling legs. I was under Tank who danced unsteadily around me—horses will try hard to avoid stepping on a person—trying to keep his footing on the treacherous incline while not tromping on me.

Several girls were off their horses trying to reach under him to pull me out, but Tank's footing was too unstable. The next thing I saw was him rolling and then sliding downhill on his side. Mercifully the ground leveled out a short distance below. The slope was thickly carpeted with tall grass and flowers which when crushed flat made a great slide for Tank's descent. Fortunately, there were few obstacles in his path and the saddle took most of the scraping and bumping. Everyone kept saying I was so lucky he didn't fall on me when he took his tumble, and that he wasn't injured except for some minor scrapes.

By the time we were reunited, he was perfectly calm. Horses are great that way. Once the danger is over, they're back to normal. I, on the other hand, wasn't too plugged in. It took me a little while before I could stand and remain standing, take Tank's reins, grab the tail of the horse ahead of me and get in line to switchback up the nightmarish slope. I don't remember anything else about that day. Concussions will do that to you. All I could do was what the early pioneers and cowboys did: pick yourself up and do what you had to do. I still have a tangible reminder of the events of the day, a bump that remains on the back of my head where that rock smacked into me.

Several years later in college I saw Ingmar Bergman's film "The Seventh Seal." When it came to one of the last scenes of the film in which Death had tied most of the characters together and with a whip drove them up a steep hill to hell, I flashed back to this day. I was struck with Bergman's juxtaposition of hell being up. Quite apt, I thought.

Tank becomes a bulldozer

My next scrape with rough ride near-disaster occurred during my second summer at the ranch on a day that wasn't supposed to be a rough ride, but a little before lunch qualified as one for me. Early that morning, we rode out of our base camp where we'd been packing out for the better part of the week. Charlie, one of the wranglers, led us up along some ridges we hadn't previously explored.

For most of the morning, we threaded through small meadows and pockets of thick brush. We eventually ended up along the edge of a cliff so steep it could only be climbed with ropes and pitons. I was at the end of the line that day also, winding up there when I stopped not only to tighten Tank's cinch but to re-adjust his saddle blanket which had slipped significantly. By the time I mounted up again I was riding with a group of girls from another cabin I didn't know well, but they all knew Tank. The story of how he acquired his nickname gave him some notoriety and by association, me. Since we were now the very last ones in line we stuck together when someone else had to tighten a cinch and a couple of others stopped to pee. When we discovered we were separated from the girls ahead of us, we called out to make contact but were too far apart to be heard.

We shortly came to what looked like a dead end. To the left was a straight drop to the valley floor. At the very top it was marginally less steep and covered with sandy shale. Directly ahead and all along our right side was and had been for some distance thick, dense, gnarly brush which was more than shoulder height to our horses and several feet deep. It blocked us from going forward or turning inland away from the edge. It looked like something maybe we girls might be able to crawl and climb over but how could we get the horses through? What path had the others taken?

I was the first to ride up to where the brush blocked our path. Tank and I stopped and I surveyed the situation. So, I noticed, did Tank. His body posture indicated he was in full study mode. He stood still with his ears pricked forward, head lowered and forward, scanning the area. I saw to the left there were several dents in the sandy shale. Had a wild animal or even the wind made those marks, or had the rest of our group gone across there I wondered? It looked far too steep and dangerous to even attempt. The other girls came forward to get a better look.

We talked about what to do. One of the traits of us girls attracted to ranch life was a willingness to bravely face the many risks such a life provided. However, uncharacteristically none of us wanted to try going across the shale.

We huddled up in a circle with our horses' heads in the center and considered our options. Trying to make it across the top of the cliff just didn't seem to be an option. We leaned toward going back the way we came to see if we'd missed a turn the others might have taken. Tensions were high and in those situations there is a tendency to throw out silly suggestions as well as practical ones.

One girl said, "Why don't we have Tank bulldoze our way through?" We all laughed.

"Great idea," I said getting into the spirit of it.

I wheeled him around and moved him forward to stand directly in front of the brush. Then I leaned forward and patted his neck, just as I'd seen Roy Rogers do to Trigger many times in the movies.

"Come on, boy. You can do it. You can get us through," channeling Roy again.

The other girls chimed in. I sat back up, now fully in the role, gave him his head and lightly touched his sides with my heels. To everyone's astonishment, especially mine, he reared up and crashed his front feet down on the brush. It cracked and broke under his hooves with surprising ease. We were all stunned, particularly me—so much so I'm surprised I stayed in the saddle. Until that time I had never seen him come close to rearing and yet here he was like a scene straight out of the movies. He wasn't rearing all the way up like Silver during the intro to "The Lone Ranger," just high enough to get some good smashing power going.

I was surprised to hear the snap of brush breaking. It was much more brittle than it had appeared from my perch on Tank's back, looking to me like a firm rubbery kind of shrub wood difficult to break. Had I first dismounted to check it out before launching into another episode of TV cowboy I might have discovered that fact. How did Tank know? Was it his 50 million years of inherited survival instincts that enabled him to discern from a few feet away what brush he could crush and what he couldn't? He didn't need to set foot on it first as I would have had to. Also his body carried a lot more crushing power than mine did and the iron shoes he wore helped.

He quickly cleared enough of a path to get us through although the horses had some minor cuts on their legs from threading through the broken branches. It didn't take long to see we were on the right trail and we soon caught up with the others who by this time had backtracked to look for us.

During lunch, we honored Tank by weaving a crown of mountain grasses and flowers to hang over his ears. In a hastily devised ceremony we knighted him Sir Bulldozer. He stood quietly throughout and at its conclusion eagerly ate the crown we offered him as his prize. As for me, I was thrilled that my TV cowboy batting average had just shot from zero to 500.

Charlie told us they had indeed gone across the shale and chided us for chickening out. He also confirmed that doubling back to look for another trail would only have taken us further away from the rest of the group and could have gotten us lost.

It didn't feel to us like we'd chickened out. There was something different about that situation, including the fact that as a unit we not only responded with caution but with growing apprehension.

Good boy!

Until piecing together the elements of this story more than 50 years later, I always ascribed the fact that we didn't go across the shale to a decision we girls made. But the truth is, I now realize, we never got to the point of making a decision. Tank did it for us. Through our tension-breaking clowning around, I gave him the opening to rescue us.

There had been many other instances up in the mountains when we had to decide which way to proceed and Tank showed no interest in the outcome, probably because there was no potential threat or high emotion regarding choice of route. However, from the time we first examined our options up on that ridge he'd gone into threat assessment mode. I believe his superior survival instincts kicked in. He had to have also been acutely aware of our indecision, moving into fear, since sensing the emotional environment is a key component of those instincts.

We were scared. I don't remember any other time at the ranch feeling that way, probably because we were in danger and more so than we could take in at the time. Perhaps that is why, over the years, my mind periodically returned to those moments on that mountain ridge, and why each time the hairs on the back of my neck stood up—and still do—whenever I think about what happened there, and what could have happened there, caught between the shale and the chaparral.

I couldn't then and cannot now shake the feeling that had Tank and I attempted to go across that shale—because we would have been the first to lead off—we would not have made it, instead plunging hundreds of feet straight down to a certain death. It doesn't matter that all the girls and their horses that took that passage earlier did so safely. I know we wouldn't have. Why else would Tank have taken such extraordinary action if survival had not been at stake? Maybe those more experienced in such matters can offer an opinion, but they weren't up on that ridge with us.

At the time of our knighting ceremony for the new Sir Bulldozer, I thought we were simply celebrating my horse performing an extraordinary act. It would be a long time before I realized it was probably also a celebration of something far greater—our lives.

When we got back to our base camp that evening, Sam came over to chat with us while we unsaddled our horses and to hear about the day's events. Several girls excitedly told him. When they finished, he called for everyone to listen up. Then he gave us absolute hell—both we who had fallen behind and those out front who hadn't checked to see if everyone was following. Afterwards he walked over to Tank and me.

He tried not to smile when he said, "I told you he was a good horse."

He then stroked Tank a few times on his neck, patted him and said, "Good boy."

So what did save me?

At this point, Sam thought it would be a good idea to move me to the head of the line on rough rides since I'd had two traumatic experiences in the back. Therefore, on the next one I went to the head of the line with him. The best laid plans, as they say.

In previous rough rides we always encountered a few really brutal uphill battles which led to other ridges and high meadows with more challenging inclines. But this time when we reached the top of the ridge, the ugly scramble to get up there suddenly seemed like a walk in the park compared to what we had to do next. We saw that the only way out of where we were was to take an even steeper grade down. The route to the bottom was covered in slippery shale scattered with large rocks and a few boulders that would make switchbacking down as a group too dangerous to attempt. There would be much skidding and even some tumbling down this one. That would be OK with just a bunch of girls, but factor in more than 45 horses, each weighing anywhere between 900 and 1300 pounds, which could make the journey down together messy. So the horses would need to precede us.

Sam told us we'd have to go down in small groups and that we six at the head of the line were going to go first with him. He instructed us to pull off the saddles and blankets and tie the ends of the reins securely to the bridles to be left on the horses. To get the horses to start their trip down we had to wave our arms or saddle blankets, swat them on their rumps, and even get behind and push as I had to do. Finally, our horses began their reluctant descent. The grade was so steep that once they got started they held their front legs more or less straight and their hind legs in an almost seated position—looking like big dogs. Because of the angle from which we watched them, we mostly saw only the tops of their heads and their big rumps bobbing as they skidded over bumps. It looked strangely as if they were mooning us.

When the ground leveled out, they quickly headed for safety in a stand of trees about 30 yards away. Once they reached the bottom, we pitched our saddles to roll down behind them. The horses never fell going down the slope. We did. Clearly it pays in those situations to have four legs instead of two. Our horses descended because they had to. So did we, but we also enjoyed it, loving to "ski" down the shale on our boots since most of us were from ski country. However it's much harder to keep your balance wearing high-heeled western boots. It was fun, yes, but if we fell, and we often did, we could lose sections of our jeans along with some skin. I left a few patches of both in those mountains.

The other girls who came down with me went into the trees to retrieve our horses while I stayed at the bottom to collect and stack the saddles and blankets so they didn't get knocked around by the next wave of horses starting their descent. Sam stood some distance away, his attention on the group above us. I had just turned toward the trees to see if the other girls and Tank were in sight when Sam yelled my name at full volume followed by, "Hit the ground!"

Before I had time to think I felt someone push me really hard between my shoulder blades. I landed flat on the ground with my face in the scratchy dirt. A loud *whumping* sound of something really heavy bounced next to me. I never saw the large boulder that landed where I'd been standing. Had I not hit the ground instantly, I would have been crushed under it. When I got up Sam's normally tan face was ashen. His voice shook as he kept saying, "Thank God. Thank God."

I became Sam's poster child for a really good camper. When we were all assembled again he told everyone that what had saved my life was my quick response to his command to hit the deck. I don't know how it happened that I did. Though my body was sprawled on the ground my mind was still standing up saying, "Huh?" The other girls down there with me had been too far away to push me. Having difficulty figuring out where that push came from I later asked each one individually if they had done it. They all said they weren't near me, some expressing surprise I even asked them.

I don't know who or what shoved me to the ground that day but whatever it was I am grateful for it. I surely would have been killed had I not moved, or in this case been moved, from where I stood. At age 14, in the midst of wild adventure, I just accepted the experience and kept moving, so the full force of what happened that day didn't hit me until many years later. The only conclusion I can come to is that some presence other than that of the other people with me at the bottom of that slope intervened because it wasn't yet my time to die.

CHAPTER 9

All About Tank

How Tank came to live at the ranch

One of the perks of a high status with Sam, which I increasingly accrued, was that two or three girls got to crowd into the big cab of the cattle truck on trips we didn't take on horseback—like into town to see a movie or to a rodeo many miles away. There were usually at least 45 of us and somehow a few of us got the distinction of riding up front more often than others. I couldn't tell you how that happened, except Sam did have his favorites.

We loved hearing Sam tell us his experiences on the ranch during seasons when we girls weren't there, or tales—some of them tragic— of year-round residents getting lost in blizzards, trapped in avalanches or landslides, or searching for lost horses and other livestock. Sam was a mesmerizing storyteller and he didn't like competition. He liked an audience and we enjoyed being his.

One day in the cab, the story turned to a cheerier note than natural disasters. Sam asked me, "Did I ever tell you the story of how Tank came to be at the ranch?"

"No!" I said, really excited. I was glad the others in the cab also wanted to hear it.

Each winter, the horses were quartered in a large pasture several miles down the valley. They were checked on periodically and hay dropped when needed late in the winter or after a blizzard. A couple of years before my first summer at the ranch, several horses got out through a collapsed part of the fence. Horses wandering around loose do not go unnoticed. After the first call from someone finding horses with his brand, Sam immediately went to check how many and which horses were missing. The word went out, easy in rural areas, to be on the lookout for them. Sam's brand and its left shoulder location were described.

All but two of the escapees were quickly found and brought home. Eventually, a call came from a man across the valley.

"I found three of your horses," he said.

He added that only two had Sam's brand but the third was sticking like glue to the others so he figured they all came from the same place. Sam drove to get them. The third horse was Tank, and as Sam started loading his two in the truck Tank had his nose practically Velcroed to the hip of one of them. He told us Tank was saying he was going where those two were going. Sam said he already liked him and told the rescuer he'd take the horse back with him and figured it was now his turn to find out who he belonged to.

It wasn't long before a man called and confirmed the third horse was his. He kept repeating how relieved and grateful he was to hear his horse was safe because, he kept saying, he was such a good horse and he really liked him. He'd been torn up the past couple of weeks trying to find him, fearing him dead. Sam expected the man to make arrangements to collect him when instead he started asking questions about the ranch.

He told Sam he was a part-time guide with many changes going on in his life and it sounded as if a girl's ranch would be a much better home for his horse. He acknowledged it was a bad situation for any horse to be alone with no other horses. He asked Sam if he'd like to keep him. Sam asked how much he wanted for him and the man, again gushing affection for his horse, said he'd be glad to just give him for free since it sounded like he would get a great home.

Sam told us since he already liked Tank and the fact that the man had been close to tears through much of their conversation indicated he didn't think the guy was trying to unload a loser horse on him. And that's how Tank came to the ranch.

Tank's herd dynamics

Horses need to be with other horses. To feel comfortable and safe they need the herd association, even if it's a small group. Tank clearly demonstrated this the way he affixed himself to the two escapees of Sam's. It probably explained why he broke out from his previous home. He was lonely.

After seeing up close and personal the importance of the herd I knew I could never own a horse and pasture it without other horses, thereby denying it the feeling of safety and companionship such company brings. I feel sad every time I see a horse quartered all alone.

Some horses at the ranch had close personal friends in the herd which made it easier in the morning for wranglers to identify who had not yet voluntarily come into the corrals from a night of grazing in the foothills. For instance, if Dakota was missing, so were Peace Pipe and Rowdy. They would always be found together. Other horses were loners in a crowd and content to be so. For them, the herd was enough. Tank appeared to be one of those. The whole time we were together he didn't buddy up with anyone else in the herd of more than 70 horses.

Because of Tank's apparent loner status and my inexperience in herd dynamics, I had concluded that perhaps Tank didn't have much status within the herd. That may have been the case my first year at the ranch, which was his second year, but those dynamics may have shifted somewhere in our second summer together. I noticed he commandeered an increasingly larger portion of the crowded corral for only him. It wasn't unusual to see Tank standing with one hind leg cocked and a good 10—15 feet of space around him. If any horse came near he needed only to pin his ears back flat (horse talk for, "I'm armed and dangerous—advance at your own risk.") and it immediately moved away.

The fact that his territorial stance went unchallenged indicated respect, and respect in herd dynamics equals dominance—not necessarily herd boss but at least higher up in the pecking order. With dominance also comes responsibility for the safety of the herd, which might further explain his actions up on that mountain ridge when he smashed us a trail through the dense brush. I would love to know what he and the other horses said to each other at that time.

Tank's Running Walk

Many of us had never ridden western style before coming to the ranch. I had been taught to ride English style on a flat saddle and to always post a trot. A trot is a two-beat gait and can be jarring to sit. "Posting a trot" consists of moving up and down in rhythm with the gait by gripping with your knees, using the stirrups to leverage that movement.

Western riding styles are based on spending all day in the saddle. So you sit the trot or jog (slow trot). Posting for long distances would be exhausting. Plus, you'd look and feel like a jack-in-the-box moving over the rugged terrain. Tank had a nice jog and I learned how to sit it without bouncing. I got good at it, but never totally caught up to the way the wranglers—the guys who were born in the saddle—always looked as though they were part of the horse.

One day my counselor, Carolyn, rode next to me and kept staring at Tank's feet. I finally asked her why.

"I think your horse can really fast walk," she answered.

I hadn't known until coming out West that a fast walk, called a running walk, was a valuable asset in a horse. The most common form I learned was when a horse trotted with its hind feet and walked with its front feet. It's a marvelous gait to ride, very smooth and a lot more restful at the end of the day than sitting a trot. If you spend all day in the saddle its value becomes evident. Plus, its pace is quite fast. Some horses did it naturally. Since Tank didn't, I would have to train him.

Carolyn showed me how to urge him forward, then gently rein him back just as he was about to break into a trot—over and over. It only took a couple of days before he needed no urging from me. I don't know if Carolyn told me she thought Tank could walk fast because she saw something I didn't or whether it was just to motivate me to try. I learned later that many Mustangs come by a running walk naturally—or with only a little encouragement. It's a throw back to their origins from the Spanish Conquistador horses that also spawned the Peruvian Paso and other fast walking breeds.

Whatever it was, it worked. It soon became evident Tank enjoyed doing it. One by one he started out-walking every fast walking horse on the ranch. It didn't take long for him to dethrone the fastest walker who had held the title for many years. Tank didn't stop there. He beat every visiting horse and I sensed his enjoyment at being reigning king of the walkers. I was so proud of him.

His fast walk became faster and he'd occasionally advance it to what I called a bunny hop—but only when he had an audience. It was faster than a walk but not quite a lope, cool to ride and comical to watch I was told. I wouldn't know because he wouldn't do it for anyone else so I could only view it from his back. I so loved that about him—something special just for the two of us.

Tank teaches me a lesson

We had taken a long day ride high up behind the ranch, exploring a new area, making our way single file along a narrow trail threading through large bushes with hard green golf ball sized balls growing at the ends of their many branches. They proved too enticing for Katie, Pam and me. We ripped them off and threw them at each other as we rode, with me getting the brunt of it since I rode between the two of them. We quickly expanded our range to others ahead of and behind us in line. I had an older brother and as a result had developed a particularly accurate throwing arm, resulting in everyone ganging up in retribution to bombard me en masse. Those balls were large and hard and stung when they hit.

We didn't pay attention to the fact our little game had taken our horses hostage. They were also getting pummeled, primarily on their rumps and heads which are particularly touchy areas. The first sign Tank was uncomfortable was when he started tossing his head. I ignored it. When he began moving his ears out sideways, twitching, I knew he was really annoyed. I ignored that sign, too. Bad call on my part.

Then he stopped. I had wrapped his reins around the horn, letting them go slack so I could use both hands to fire off return volleys. I thought he might have interpreted this as a lack of direction from me. I urged him forward but he didn't move. Instead he turned his head all the way around and glared at me. I was startled—he had fire in his eyes and clearly was angry. I had never seen a look like that coming from him.

I realized Katie—riding immediately behind me—had seen it, too, when I heard her say, "Wow! That was some look!"

He had fired a warning shot across my bow that needed heeding. I'd like to say we stopped the game then and there, but no, unfortunately, we didn't. It took a few more minutes before Katie and I initiated getting the word up and down the line to stop it. A little belatedly, I apologized to Tank for my thoughtlessness. Well, that's the end of that, I thought. I was wrong.

We soon stopped for lunch in a Munchkin-sized valley with really steep sides to it. The valley was so small there was barely enough room for 45 girls to sit on the ground to eat and for the horses to spread out sufficiently to have enough room to graze. Since Tank didn't wander when saddled and bridled, I didn't keep my eye on him. When lunch was over we went to collect our horses. Everyone quickly got her horse except me. Tank was nowhere to be found.

At that point I was more puzzled than concerned. Several others joined in the search, making slow 360-degree turns scanning up and down the sides of this tiny pocket in the mountainside. Suddenly Sandy burst out laughing so hard all she could do was point to a small clump of trees a little ways up the slope. Then we all saw it—the brief flash of something red behind a small, but dense, cluster of trees. It was Tank's tail. The stand of trees was thick enough to hide his body, but it wasn't quite wide enough to conceal its length. I then saw his head, which was turned and looking at me. To hide from me that rascal had scaled the slope I then struggled to climb. It was so steep I sometimes needed to steady myself by reaching forward to grab handfuls of the sturdy, tough grass that grew there.

I marveled at the stealth with which he had gone into hiding. He continued to watch me, and as my relation to his position changed, he shifted accordingly trying to remain concealed. When I reached him he surrendered, resigned that his period of invisibility had ended. I held onto his reins and side-by-side we awkwardly threaded and slipped our way down.

How had he gotten up there without anyone noticing? The general consensus was that all eyes had been on the only two viable exits—the way we came in and the exit on the opposite side. Everyone thought it was very funny and I had to admire Tank's cleverness. He had made quite a statement. I again apologized to him for not recognizing the painful impact of our game and the disrespect shown him—by me in particular.

He likes me! He really likes me!

Only Sam and the wranglers were authorized to go into the corrals in the morning to bridle horses. The reason, Sam told us, was that he wanted to prevent girls not so skilled at catching and bridling horses from bungling the job which could make the horse "head shy" about being bridled. This rule applied even to those of us who were skilled in these tasks, although out on pack trips we were free to catch and bridle our own horses. The exception to this rule was if your horse was already head shy, then you could bridle your own horse.

These rules made no sense to me until I started reasoning through them. What Sam was trying to accomplish, I realized, was two fold: First, get the horses caught and bridled as quickly a possible so everyone could get saddled up and headed out for the day. Second, prevent injuries resulting from more than 40 girls milling around the already tight space of the corral with horses some of which would just as soon kick you as look at you. If your horse was already head shy, it would take longer for Sam or the wranglers to bridle and would slow down the efficiency of the process.

Tank was easy to bridle until one day during my second summer at the ranch, seemingly no different from the ones before it. When Sam tried to bridle him, he tossed his head, backed away and snorted. We were surprised. Did he have an injury to his head? Close examination revealed nothing physical that would make his head touchy. After a bit of a struggle Tank was bridled. He repeated his performance the next two days. The following morning Sam started to walk toward him in the corral and stopped as Tank backed away from him. He looked at Tank, looked at me, and back at Tank. Then he tossed his bridle to me.

"Here," he said. "I think he wants you to bridle him."

I entered the corral and walked up to my horse. He lowered his head and helpfully slipped it into his bridle. Sam just shook his head and laughed. That was the last of Tank's head shyness. He was a clever boy.

Food, glorious food!

Tank's most excellent caper, however, was his occupation of the alfalfa field. It was a relatively small field, the size ranchers and farmers use to grow feed for their own livestock not for commercial sale. Unfortunately, the field was in a neighboring ranch, immediately adjacent to the road we took from the ranch to the highway. Each morning during the last few weeks of our last summer together the sun rose, the air warmed, and the birds sang—all to witness Tank happily munching alfalfa in the middle of a field that wasn't Sam's.

Tank's eating the neighbor's alfalfa could potentially create a serious problem between ranchers. I'm not sure how Sam and the other rancher resolved it—probably money exchanged hands—but Tank continued to help himself to the alfalfa.

No one could figure out how he got in there. Sam, the other rancher, the wrangler we had that summer, and I patrolled the fence but couldn't find an entry spot. The most logical bet, everyone concluded, was that he somehow rolled under the fence, but we couldn't find any place that looked likely. Horses do not gracefully roll under fences, nor do they do so without leaving quite a trail. There were no holes in the fence either.

Alfalfa is a rich hay, so rich it isn't healthy for a horse to eat a lot of it. Plus it puts weight on an animal. Tank's girth was beginning to swell from his nightly indulgences. One morning as I again led Brer Rabbit out of his briar patch, our wrangler, who was still trying to find Tank's entrance point, laughed, slapped him on his growing belly and declared, "One thing I know for sure. He's not jumping in!"

The mystery wasn't solved before I left for home, if it ever was solved. As for Tank not jumping in—I'm not entirely certain he didn't. He had proven himself capable of great strategy when special action was required. And there was a small steep hill very close to that field. But the idea of my sturdy Tank flying through the air—I just don't know. Still …

Déjà Vu

There were experiences I had and sensations I felt only when I was with Tank. They didn't happen all that frequently, but when they did I was carried to a time and place far from where I physically stood. I didn't discuss this with anyone until years later. Not because I felt it was secret, but because I didn't know how to talk about it, nor did I feel a need to.

Sometimes up in the mountains I'd stop to look out over the valley's expanse, feeling a oneness with this magnificent place in which—for brief moments—I could see through the veneer of 20th century roads and buildings below to a time long before they existed. These experiences weren't anything I could conjure. They only happened with Tank.

One morning during my first summer, the girls in my cabin and I explored the foothills behind the ranch where several creeks threaded through the aspens. We got into a game of wild chase as fast as the terrain would allow—leaping over creeks, crashing between trees, making sharp twisting turns on the steep slopes until suddenly we burst into a small clearing.

We all immediately stopped when we saw we were in a cemetery, a very old one. The sunlight filtering through the fluttering aspen leaves cast the area in dappled gold. I later pieced together from others that there were about 20 crude rotting wooden grave markers. Nearly all the names and dates were still legible. The strange part was that only women and young children were buried there—no men. Furthermore, the markers recorded they all died within a short time span of less than two years.

During those moments I couldn't move. Frozen in the saddle, I was aware the other girls had dismounted and walked among the graves for closer looks. They excitedly called to each other but I could barely hear them. It was like when I was a young child and had a high fever. I was aware of my parents talking to me and each other, but what they said seemed to come from such a far away place—and I was in an entirely different place.

Not only could I not move, Tank didn't move. He didn't try to graze, as he normally would have. He had stopped in front of three graves—and there he stood and there I sat staring at the markers that told me a young woman and her two children lay buried beneath them. They had died within a few weeks of each other. Those three graves were the only ones I really saw.

Finally, we returned to the ranch but it took me the better part of the day to return to being present. I was left with a growing feeling that strengthened over the years that one of the graves I looked down at as I sat on Tank's back was *my* grave—a grave from a former life. I feel that with a certainty I can't prove, but I continue to feel it nonetheless. It also gives me a greater understanding of my strong pull to the West—both past and present.

I have no explanation for Tank's behavior except to offer that perhaps he, too, was there with me in that life. Whatever it was during our time in the small decaying cemetery, he and I shared it on a different plane than the one we stood on.

Chapter 10

Our First Separation

My parents see my dream in action

Instead of taking the train back to Chicago with everyone else at the end of my first summer at the ranch, my parents drove out to take me home. They arrived a week before I was to leave so we could have some time together of my showing them around the area.

They weren't expected until morning but decided to drive out to the ranch the evening before, arriving as it started to get dark towards the end of one of my evening road wrangling assignments. We had driven the herd off the highway and were halfway down the long dusty ranch road. We needed to get the horses past a large field and through the ranch gate that eventually led to the foothills where they would graze and sleep. The field was fenced on the far side, which prevented the horses from a more direct route to the foothills, but that didn't stop them from trying. Every now and then some of them would make a break for it. I remember that evening as just another time they tried a jailbreak. It happened on the side I was responsible for so Tank and I took off, jumping an irrigation ditch to get to where we could turn them back.

Mom and Dad made the turn onto the ranch road behind us just as this happened. As Dad tells it—and it's much better than it actually happened—he saw these horses break from the herd. Then this girl

63

quickly "spurred her horse into action" (none of us wore spurs) so he was running "belly to the ground fast" (well . . maybe) and then "sailed over an irrigation ditch" (yes!) to intercept the horses, quickly turning them back to where they needed to be.

They didn't know it was me. It was nearly dark, they'd never seen Tank, I had a dark tan; and what had been short hair 10 weeks earlier when I left home was now shaggy and blowing all over. It wasn't until they parked the car and walked over to the corrals where I unsaddled Tank that we connected. Dad was thrilled. He told me I looked just like a western girl working on her ranch. He said it was the experience he hoped I would have. Even though I'd described some of my wrangling experiences in my letters, he said it was good to witness it firsthand.

The painful goodbye

I had spent 11 weeks at the ranch and it was over way too soon. I dreaded leaving. I knew from my previous camp experiences that leaving your friends at the end of camp was painful enough, but this was the first time I had to leave my horse as well. It was excruciating.

The idea of leaving Tank made my heart hurt—my actual heart. Up until that moment, I'd always thought the expression "broken heart" was merely symbolic of the pain of separation and loss. Now I realized how physical that pain could be.

When the dreaded, last day came I wrapped myself around his neck and sobbed into his mane. Mom and Dad had to pry me off him to get me into the car. I knelt in the back seat like a five year old, looking out the rear window long after I couldn't see Tank anymore. I cried all the way to South Dakota my parents told me. They kept assuring me I'd see him again the following summer. It didn't help.

My chrysalis stage

I went through quite a transformation between my first and second summers at the ranch.

I dramatically changed my after school TV viewing habits. Most afternoons instead of watching cowboys on their horses racing across the TV screen, my friends and I danced to the hits of the day brought into our homes by Dick Clark and his pop singer guests on American Bandstand.

I discovered the mirror. In its reflection I could catch occasional glimpses of a prettiness that would take a frustratingly long time to materialize. My braces were removed and I realized I liked my smile. I grew my hair long and experimented with different styles, resorting to the fallback ponytail when my styling attempts bombed. I discovered boys, but it would be quite a while before they discovered me.

Mom and Dad helped me upgrade my bedroom to something reflecting my rapidly developing teenage tastes. Never interested in such things before, I jumped into this process enthusiastically, surprising my parents and me. I chose a palette of white and red, starting with twin Hollywood-style beds covered with white, quilted Chenille spreads with scalloped edges that came just to the dust ruffles. I was most proud of the large, round, red furry rug that covered most of the floor, spending hours lying on it reading or listening to music.

Dad's contribution was a big (he did nothing small) bulletin board he built for me. The bed I chose to sleep in was against the wall under the bulletin board. The first item I pinned to it was a coiled ring of dark, red hair I'd taken from Tank's tail and tied wreath-like with a ribbon. I put this precious memento fairly low down so when lying in bed I could reach up and run my fingers over its wiry smoothness. I'd wonder how Tank was doing in the deep, cold snow of the Rockies, and tried to imagine him in his shaggy winter coat he would shed long before I'd see him again. I warmed myself with thoughts of when we would soon be together.

CHAPTER 11

Betrayal, Hard Truths and Lessons

A problem of image

The following summer, I stepped off the train in the West and easily stepped back into my role as a working ranch girl. I was so excited to be with Tank again. I threw my arms around his neck, nestled into his mane and kissed him on his cheek, grateful to be back again in his big, wonderful presence.

My parents wrote and told me Sam sent glowing reports about what a great girl I was and how I contributed to and was getting the most out of my ranch experience.

However, trouble was brewing, created completely by me and, unfortunately, undetected by me.

I didn't recognize at the time how I increasingly projected onto Tank the rapidly evolving body and image consciousness I started developing that winter. Side by side with my deep affection for him was my desire for the really exciting horse I'd hoped to get when I first arrived at the ranch—an itch with a greater longing to be scratched than I realized. I was not conscious of both realities operating at the same time, let alone that they were on a collision course.

One day I rummaged around in a large bin in the barn where extra tack was stored, looking for something for Tank. Maybe a new bridle would give him some sparkle. Digging through the tangle of leather I eventually surfaced with a nice breastplate. The tooling was lovely and its stain was an exact match to his saddle. I dug further and found a matching tie-down (Easterners would call it a martingale) that attached at one end to the breastplate and the other end to the bridle's chinstrap. On most horses these additions would look rather elegant and would also indicate the horse was so spirited it needed the added restraint. Most horses, but not all.

A few days later we packed out to a remote site for several days. Tank and I were among the few who would wrangle the horses there. This was also the day I had chosen as Tank's new tie-down debut. When the wranglers saw us, they nearly fell out of their saddles laughing.

"Hey," one of them called to the other, "I've seen a lot of tie-downs, but I've never seen a tie-*up* before."

They were right. On Tank it was rather pointless since he naturally held his head low, and when he walked really fast he held it even lower. It did look pretty ridiculous and I detached it quickly. When I came to my senses, I realized that because we did so many rough and risky things he needed to have free range of motion of his head and neck. I would never shake that memory of him rolling and sliding downhill the summer before. So the tie-down went back in the tack bin, but the breastplate looked great and stayed. It also helped keep the saddle from slipping on those steep uphill climbs.

However, my longing for a horse that really needed a tie-down continued to increase. I was soon to learn the truth of Oscar Wilde's statement, a favorite of Dad's: "When the gods want to punish us, they answer our prayers."

Toward the end of the summer Sam came back to the ranch late one afternoon with a couple of horses he had just bought, a three-year-old bay mare and a two-year-old pinto gelding. The mare was a nice looking bay, purchased for one of the counselors whose horse had been injured. The pinto was rangy and not in any good proportions. He had a giraffelike neck and his head was disproportionately small—so were his ears. His legs were very long and his body short. There was no natural saddle in his spine. He was also walleyed. These are not good indicators of a quality horse.

And I wanted him—badly

The next day I asked Sam if I could have the pinto the following summer. He didn't say anything at first. Finally he just said, "No," turned and walked away.

I followed him to ask why not, saying it would be fun to train him. More silence from Sam. Then he told me, and not at all in a nice way, that he was surprised I wanted that horse because clearly it wasn't a good horse and the only reason he took him was because he and the mare were a package deal, fortunately not an expensive one. He said he was going to unload him as soon as possible, which turned out to be a couple of days later.

I remembered the discussion my parents and I had with Sam the winter before I came to the ranch, so I knew it was possible to get a new horse. Just before the summer ended I told Sam I wanted a new horse the following summer. He tried to talk me out of it, but I wouldn't hear of it. I was obsessed. Just before I left for home he said if I still wanted a different horse next year I could have one, but he wanted me to think about it over the winter.

I did think about it, but not with introspection. Any consideration I gave to the special richness of Tank's and my relationship was eclipsed by the excitement I felt at the prospect of getting a new, highly spirited horse. I wrote Sam in the early spring that I was prepared to give up Tank for a new horse. It would take time and heartbreak to understand what a rotten decision that was.

I wasn't dating yet and didn't recognize that from Tank's and my relationship emerged the first indicators of what would be my troubling pattern with men for many years—one in which I would suddenly dump a growing relationship with a nice, smart, stable, dependable guy in favor of someone new and different. "New and different" in this case equated to exciting and desirable to me. Personal qualities of excellence didn't seem to factor into these decisions, and, in fact, were painfully absent I would eventually realize. It took me many years and some disastrous relationships to recognize and come to terms with this pattern.

But these insights were too far in my future to keep Tank and me together at the beginning of my third summer. When I arrived at the ranch my new horse hadn't yet been purchased, so Sam told me to ride whatever horse wasn't spoken for.

Tank was given to another girl. She wasn't in my cabin so our paths didn't cross much, except on pack trips and rough rides. I was vaguely aware that I kept as much distance as possible between the two of them and me. However, the area where we all groomed and saddled our horses was relatively small, so I did notice she seemed to really care for Tank and fawned over him, feeding him lots of oats which I'm sure he loved. I felt a few jealousy jabs and was actually angry the first time I saw her bouncing around on his back as he jogged along, his running walk a thing of the past—just where I had left him.

Seeing what I wanted to see

Soon Sam took me to visit three different horse traders in a town quite a distance away. I didn't see any horse of interest at the first two places. By the time we got to the third, I was beginning to feel uncharacteristically co-dependent about being so picky, of taking up so much of Sam's time. I only remember him being this accommodating a couple of times before about buying a girl a new horse. I felt honored I was one.

By the time we drove onto the last trader's property I'd made up my mind I would find my horse here—lucky for the trader because I'm not sure how else he might have unloaded the horse on which I cast all my projections.

She was a dark bay, a color I'd always had a weakness for. She was quite spirited, which is how I chose to view her then. Later, I realized she was nuts. I took her on a test ride. My first clue should have been that she didn't settle down, frequently jumping sideways as I rode her. Her gaits were fairly rough, but I ignored that too. She broke into a foaming sweat shortly after I got in the saddle and threw her head a lot, showering me with her lather. Riding the crest of my obsession for something new, I ignored much of what I knew about what constituted a good horse and told Sam she would do fine. We loaded her in the truck and went back to the ranch.

Now I had a horse that really needed a tie-down so I dug it out of the tack bin. She didn't walk; she danced which got old with me real fast. Getting her to settle down so I could train her to the running walk was out of the question. I could barely get her to go straight ahead without jigging sideways, which inspired Shannon to suggest I name her Tequila, after a popular song at the time. It stuck.

Reality

A couple of days later we made a 30-plus miles trek on horseback to our base camp. Tequila danced the entire way with both of us dripping in her sweat. I was both miserable and exhausted riding her. The only good thing I can say about myself during this whole unhappy episode is I realized this was a situation entirely of my making. At least I owned that. However, it took me much longer to recognize the irony of my willingness to remain faithful to a horse I'd grown to dislike after so easily casting aside a horse I loved.

When we got to our camp that night and I unsaddled her, I was shocked to see she had developed a large cinch sore. I was always very careful about cinching a horse, making sure the skin was smoothed down so it didn't bunch up getting pinched and rubbed raw. I went to Sam for some ointment, as was the protocol when the sore was big. He wasn't happy. Cinch sores were one of his pet peeves so a lot of attention was given to preventing them. I could keep riding her as long as the sore was protected.

Whenever a horse had a cinch sore, and they were infrequent, we used sanitary napkins as soft bandages, a novel solution that could only come from a girls' ranch. I'll never forget the first time Ben examined the white cotton and gauze combo we wrapped around a cinch. When he figured out what it was, his face flushed scarlet and he actually stammered. For once, he was at a total loss for words. Those guys had to admit they really worked and occasionally came around asking for "one of those cinch sore bandages."

I salved up Tequila before turning her loose for the night and the next morning wrapped a "bandage" around her cinch in that area. That evening when I unsaddled her, the sore was huge. I was crying when I called Sam over to show him. I told him I'd been so careful and I didn't know why it had happened. The day before he'd merely been unhappy with me. Now he was angry and yelled. I felt terrible for that, but worse because she was my horse to care for and I took that responsibility seriously, even if I had discovered what a pain in the neck she was to ride. She was a big, warm, living being suffering from something that wasn't her fault, but one both Sam and I felt was mine. The sore had become so bad she couldn't be ridden until it healed.

There were always extra horses so I took potluck until the sore healed, at which time Sam cinched her up. Later that day when he checked her he found an enormous sore again. He muttered something about this was more than a cinch sore and I was told to continue to ride whoever I wanted that wasn't assigned to another girl.

Tequila was checked out by a vet who diagnosed an untreatable blood disease. They had to put her down. I felt miserable about it, hating to see any horse destroyed. But I would be less than honest if I didn't admit I also felt relief, delivered from the consequences of my skewed decision making process.

CHAPTER 12

Tank Rescues Me

Remorse sets in

Late one afternoon after the horses were released for the night, instead of going up behind the ranch to graze in the foothills, some of them bolted through the front gate before we were able to close it and headed out the road to the highway. I was still down at the corrals when this happened so Sam called to me to throw a bridle on anything I could catch and bring those horses back. There were a few horses close by, one of which was Tank. "Why not?" I thought.

We weren't supposed to ride a horse that belonged to another girl without her consent, but Sam had just given me permission to grab any horse for this brief assignment. I quickly bridled Tank and swung up on his back. The familiarity of being there felt wonderful. After seeing him jog with his new girl friend for the past few weeks, I expected that's what he would do with me, too. To my amazement, as soon as I touched him with my heels he took off doing his fast running walk. I was so pleased he hadn't forgotten—either me or his fast walk.

For the first time since turning him in for a newer, more exciting model, I began to feel the painful consequences of my decision. I was so inexperienced in dealing with that kind of situation that I had no idea how to address it, let alone atone for the guilt and remorse starting to seep in around the edges. I'd always apologized to him before when

I'd acted stupidly, or at least when I realized I had. Apologizing to an animal when you're in the wrong makes a difference I'd discovered, just as it does with humans. But I couldn't take that step toward him because it all seemed so big. My actions were too hard for me to face, let alone understand.

A message from the heart of a storm

Life has a way of constellating experiences so the painful lessons and the gifts revealed in learning them are woven together in ways that can never be imagined beforehand. A few days later a powerful storm blew into the valley arriving just at nightfall. It arrived quickly, the way storms do in the mountains. To this day, I have never experienced a night like that one.

Normally on moonless nights with so little surrounding civilization, the star-filled sky cast its own light. But not that night. The clouds were so thick and it was so dark that we could only see silhouetted outlines of forms.

The wind howled eerily and blew in rapidly changing patterns. First it battered your face and then twisted around and hit you from the back, only to change again. There was no rain yet, so enormous walls and swirls of dust were kicked up, filling the air. The combination of the elements unnerved everyone, humans and animals.

The horses had been quartered in the front pasture that evening instead of turned loose in the foothills. Early the next morning some of us were to drive them down the road to a larger pasture where they would stay during the time we would be at a rodeo in another state for three days. This would save us time the next morning instead of first having to wrangle them down from the foothills.

Sam called us all down to the corrals since a potentially dangerous situation was developing, requiring a change of plans. The front pasture was fenced with barbed wire. As the winds got stronger, the horses became agitated, aggravated by the fact that the pasture was relatively small. When horses get spooked they try to run away, which in worst case can escalate to crashing into fences. They were already restless from the storm and made snorting sounds and high-pitched squeals you don't hear horses make unless they're nervous and scared.

Sam told us he wanted our help getting them out of the pasture and moving them up into the foothills where there were no fences so they could spread out to find their own shelter. There was only one route he wanted them to take and that was through the corral area. He didn't want them running up by the cabins, dining hall and staff sleeping quarters because there were several small footbridges over the creeks that ran through the ranch that could not hold horses running across them. So he called us down to the corrals to form the only corridor he wanted the horses to take.

We formed a long line from the pasture gate through the open parts of the corral area. Our line constituted one side of the corridor and the interconnected corrals and barn made up the other side. Standing close to each other, we'd have to wave our arms or give a powerful shove to a passing shoulder or rump to keep the horses moving in the right direction. After much chaos, the first horses finally started moving through this corridor to the foothills and those immediately behind them began to follow, but it was still pretty wild.

Normally when you see horses moving together there is a steady, shared bobbing rhythm to their head movements. That night, however, horses were jinking in every direction with the added eerie quality of it being so dark we could only see them in silhouette.

Something close by caught my eye in the jumbled stream of horses. It was the steady bobbing of a horse's head and that horse headed toward me. When it stopped inches from me, I saw it was Tank. I was stunned. He lowered his head and gently touched his face to my chest. Whether he meant to touch me or was jostled by other horses I'll never know, but I thought my heart would physically burst through my ribs. I threw my arms around his neck and started to beg his forgiveness for being so selfish, so insensitive. But in the midst of my gushing, the horses behind him pushed into him and he was gone.

At first I babbled to myself that I hadn't gotten to finish my apology. Then I realized his actions said it wasn't necessary. He had just told me in his language that he chose me—character imperfections and all. He had shown me his pure and shining heart. I wish mine had been its equal.

I can never fully describe the emotional impact of that moment. It remains one of the most intimate exchanges of my life. It was also brief, as I have found true intimacy to be. The girls on either side of me who witnessed it were amazed. Had he made contact that same way walking across a corral or a pasture, his actions wouldn't have had nearly the power. It would have just seemed sweet. It was astounding horse behavior given the circumstances. In the midst of horse spook, he chose to single me out, to let me know that I was special to him.

After the events of the night calmed down I asked Sam if I could have Tank as my horse in the second session, a request he granted. The following week the first session girls departed and Tank and I were reunited.

CHAPTER 13

Paradise Lost

The game changer

Together again I consciously appreciated Tank, grateful for every day I had with him. I'm thankful I didn't know then I would never see him after that summer, even though my parents and Sam and I at the time planned on me being at the ranch the following summer. I never could have imagined the events of the next few weeks that would prevent my return. But for a few short weeks Tank and I were together.

Sam had always been playful and at times joined in our roughhousing with each other. Whereas no one thought any of his behavior was out of line, it all changed one morning. It happened after breakfast in the dining hall when announcements about the day were made.

Sam stood up, already red in the face, saying how angry he was about accusations that he roughhoused with us so he could touch our breasts. I was too shocked to take in much of what he said after that opener. I don't think anyone moved, even though he ranted on for some time.

If I had to point to one moment when I left childhood forever it would be that one.

After leaving the dining hall we talked in small groups about how shocked we all were, struggling to digest what we had just heard, to find words for processing the pummeling we'd received. Sam's ranting at breakfast ripped the covers off how we had always viewed him, giving us permission to speak out loud about what we now saw unmasked. What did it mean? Was it really true? What prompted his outburst? How come none of us—that we knew of—had heard anything about this until now?

When we started comparing notes we agreed that Sam had become a lot touchier that summer, angrily snapping at many of the girls, even turning on some of his favorites—publicly criticizing them for some minor infraction or freezing them out. Those he turned on were hurt and confused by his abrupt changes in his treatment of them. In our discovery process we found that most of us had noticed this change but had no context to explain it. All we knew was that his dining room declarations and accusations shattered the outer face of the Sam we knew—or thought we knew.

The following afternoon, Shannon and I started a conversation that extended, off and on, into the next day and night and would result in changing everything for the two of us at the ranch. These examinations further led to Shannon's and my openly acknowledging the gradual changes in Sandy over the summer. She was always quieter than Shannon or I, but this was different. She had become more and more withdrawn, even with us. Was this connected with Sam in some way?

We both wished that Katie and Pam were there, but unfortunately they had only been at the ranch during the first session of the summer. Katie in particular was a good friend of Sandy's, too, so had she been there she would have been a vital contributor to that discussion.

The truth comes out

Late the following night after everyone else was asleep, Shannon and I cornered Sandy in the bathhouse, the scene of many truth-speaking-come-to-Jesus sessions at a girl's camp. We told her we had no idea what was going on with her except that something was wrong, that we were her friends and wanted to help, even if the only thing we could do was listen.

Sandy stood by the row of sinks staring down at the floor, occasionally shaking her head. She didn't say anything for a long time. Finally, she broke down and told us Sam had been molesting her all summer while they ran errands together in the truck, explored a new trail or whenever he could get her alone. So far it hadn't been rape but it didn't have to be to have a devastating impact. Shannon and I were stunned beyond adjectives. Even though we never discovered what specifically prompted Sam's dining room outburst, Sandy had just confirmed his guilt in spite of his claims of innocence.

Sandy said she felt relieved to finally tell someone. However, she said she also felt helpless to do anything about it, afraid no one would believe her. Since we struggled with it, too, we agreed. We had no template. After all, this was the 1950s. We said we'd try to protect her but none of us really knew what that looked like except to keep the three of us together as much as possible.

Soon we were on another pack trip. Shannon and I were hyper-vigilant since Betty hadn't come on this trip. The first night out, as planned, we flanked Sandy everywhere we went. Just at dark as we all headed for our sleeping bags, Sam, who slept some distance from the rest of us, called Sandy over. He laughed and patted the top of his sleeping bag. Earlier in the summer such a gesture would have meant nothing to me. Now it gave me the creeps. Sandy turned and with her head down started to walk toward him. Though I was shocked by her robotic compliance, I intercepted her, grabbed her hand and pulled her around. Shannon quickly took her other hand.

I looked directly at Sam and said, "No, Sandy, you come with us."

Those words shot out of my mouth. I didn't know where the courage came from to stand up to Sam. The look in his eyes back at me was murderous. That exchange of only a few seconds between Sam and me remains as vivid in my mind today as the night it happened over 50 years ago.

We got Sandy back to her sleeping bag which the three of us had strategically placed between Shannon's and mine. We thought Sandy would be safe for the time being. Sam would not be able to come get her without waking us. Fortunately we would be packing out for a few more days, which made it harder for Sam to get her alone than if we'd been back at the ranch.

We managed to keep her close to us the rest of the pack trip, and at quite a price. It quickly became apparent that the good will between Sam and me was gone. He was so cold and abrupt with me that several girls asked me what happened. Since Sam had noticeably turned on others during the course of the summer—both campers and counselors—I just said I was as puzzled as they were.

Over the next few days I realized Sam wasn't outwardly going to attack me. I had a reputation for being pretty direct and outspoken and I'm sure he watched to see if I would say anything to my parents or the other girls. However, it never occurred to me to say anything to anyone. I didn't want to "out" the whole miserable situation. I instinctively knew it was way too big for me to handle. So, as is the case in much sexual abuse, silence protected the abuser. Shannon and I just wanted to protect our friend, so we continued to keep her as close as possible. Shannon, meanwhile, suffered the same fate I did with Sam.

I think another reason Sam left me alone, probably the primary reason, was he knew I could potentially be real trouble for him. I knew many of the intricacies of running a camp because my family was in the camping business, too. They ran a private girl's camp back in Wisconsin. He and I had discussed it several times, particularly on that long trip we took together the summer before on the day we got Tequila. The biggest sources of referrals are campers, their parents and other camp directors. It wouldn't do to get tough with someone who could potentially cause him trouble, especially someone who had connections with other camp directors who were a very tight group.

I was knowledgeable enough in behind-the-scenes camp operations to be certain that Sam would find some coded way to let my parents know I was no longer welcome at the ranch. I just didn't know what form the message would take, only that it would probably arrive home before I did. I'd have to wait until then to find out how he expressed it. I also felt fairly safe that he wouldn't chew me up too badly because Mom and Dad would push to know from both of us what precipitated such a dramatic reversal from Sam's and my repeated glowing reports about my camp experience. After all, there had been talk of my continuing to come back as a camper and to return as a counselor once I was in college.

CHAPTER 14

Goodbye

Tank's and my sunset days

During my last couple of weeks at the ranch Sam's anger at me was palpable. Used to being open about things, I felt increasingly walled off from the other girls because I couldn't share with them the reason for his obvious coldness towards me.

Unfortunately, in spite of our efforts Shannon and I weren't completely successful at keeping Sam from Sandy. The dark, heavy unwanted presence of sexual abuse opened a gulf that began to separate us from each other. We didn't know what to do, how to protect Sandy, how to be with each other.

There was one warm, sunny place—Tank. I still had him and the precious time I spent with him. There was something so calming, so healing about being in the aura of his instinctive consciousness that dealt only with the reality of what is. When my soul ached he patiently stood by me and accepted my clinging embraces, my tears running down his neck as I hung on to him, seeking the comfort he naturally provided.

In the short time left, Tank and I alone, sometimes joined by a couple of other girls and their horses slipped away, riding to favorite hideaways and special places discovered over the past summers. We were supposed to always let someone know where we were but at that point I didn't, following one of my Dad's favorite expressions: "May as well be hung for a sheep as a lamb." I didn't think Sam would interfere and he didn't.

I had to leave before camp ended that summer because of family plans, which meant I would have to ride the train to Chicago alone. Sam would be my chauffeur on the long drive to the train stop. He wisely planned to take along someone else—a real chatterbox. That was fine with me. She'd be a much needed buffer.

I didn't want any of the clinging goodbyes I'd gone through leaving Tank and the ranch my previous two summers. Since we had to leave really early in the morning to catch the train, I decided not to go to bed at all. I spent the entire night hanging out with Tank. I talked to him a lot. I cried, sometimes my face buried in his mane, other times just sitting on the ground. I held my cheek next to his and listened to his rhythmic chewing. I lay on my back on his back, my head on his rump—no saddle or bridle—content to go where he went as he grazed. It was a magnificent night and as I looked up at the stars I wondered when I'd ever be this close to them again.

Throughout the night and into the early morning other girls came out to join us for a bit. We sang our favorite songs over and over—including the one with the verse "… tie my bones to his back, turn our faces to the west…"

At dawn I went back to the cabin to change into my "city" clothes and to stuff my boots, jeans and Levi jacket into my trunk. Tank, I shortly learned, went for dessert. As we drove through the ranch gate there he was in the alfalfa field again. I silently thanked him for that, for making my last view of him one that made me laugh.

The long ride home

It was a long sad train ride back to Chicago. I was beyond tears. I remember little of that 30-hour trip except leaning my head against the window, watching the landscape of the West slip into my past and feeling my heart hurt so deeply that nothing could reach it to heal the pain. Tank was gone—forever gone. I'd never see him again. I was in such a dark place I couldn't even fantasize about how I could come back for him sometime in the future. My ranching paradise also was gone – also forever.

When I got back home the first thing my father wanted to know was what happened that summer. I asked him what he meant, knowing full well what he meant. He told me Sam had written them it was his opinion I had gotten the most out of my camping experience there, and while I had been quite an asset in the past he felt I would benefit more next summer from a different camping experience. If you're in the camping business, that's code for death.

I told Dad, "Maybe he's right," and deflected him by talking about coming back to camp in Wisconsin next summer.

I learned much later he didn't buy my explanation, but he didn't press me. We both knew I was pretty hard to get information out of when I didn't want to talk. He left the subject alone until more than 20 years later during one of my visits to him and Mom in their retirement home in the Southwest. I had driven somewhere with Dad one night while he ran an errand.

We'd been talking about innocuous things when he suddenly turned to me and asked, "What happened that last summer at the ranch?"

I remember thinking how grateful I was it was night so he couldn't clearly see my face, but I told him the truth.

He said, "My God, why didn't you tell me?"

I answered, "I didn't think you'd believe me."

"Well," he admitted, "you're probably right."

I did tell one other person, my best friend, Anne, about what Sam did to Sandy. She knew them both since she had also come to the ranch with me part of my first summer. She didn't believe me. There wasn't anything else to say about it. None of us knew how to discuss sexual abuse. There was no public dialogue about it other than "stay away from strangers," not very helpful when the culprit was someone known and trusted by all of us.

When we were in college Sam invited Anne to be a counselor at the ranch. When she returned home the end of that summer, the first thing she told me was that now she believed me. Not catching the beginning of the thread, I told her I didn't know what she meant. She said she now believed what I'd told her Sam did to Sandy, "because he did it to me."

CHAPTER 15

Paradise Regained

Can't appreciate heaven without knowing hell

After that summer I never initiated any contact with Sandy or Shannon and they never communicated with me. Katie and I stayed in touch for a while, but I didn't tell her about Sam's abuse of Sandy. I didn't think it was mine to tell.

That first winter was hell for me. I had no one to talk with about it. My pain of losing Tank was deep and sharp, and I kept pushing it away. At first he constantly came into my thoughts, but I couldn't hold him there for long. Though I ached to welcome him I just couldn't—I couldn't look at him full on. It always hurt too much to feel him close, to think about him.

The fact that I hadn't yet acknowledged and understood the pattern driving my callous discard of him at the end of our second summer together and my guilt about it made it easier to dissociate and shove his memory into a more manageable place—a place, I eventually realized, that also walled me off from comfort or resolution. When I got into my 30s I knew he had to be dead and I pushed him far away where he stayed for many years.

Another game changer saves me

A few years ago I rediscovered the only surviving picture of Tank and me. My father had plucked it from a pile of photos taken my last summer at the ranch and had it framed. Over the years I noticed it was in his den but I never really saw it—I had become that insulated from Tank. A few years after my parents died I started rummaging through the many cartons of their personal papers and other belongings I'd taken home and stored in our garage. In sorting through them I eventually found that photo.

For the first time since leaving the ranch I didn't shut Tank out. In fact, I laughed as the memory of when the photo was taken rushed back. It was only a few days before I left the ranch forever. I'd led Tank up to the expanse of lawn by the cabins to have friends take a couple of pictures of us against a green background instead of the pale bare dirt of the corral area. We talked about where I should stand but Tank made that decision. He came up to my side from behind, put his head over my shoulder and stood there—a perfect Kodak moment captured.

Had he walked up to me face to face and put his head over my shoulder it would have been a sign of disrespect—like, "I don't see you, you don't count, and I have already gone past you." But what he did that day was quietly come up from behind and simply stand next to me—very companionable.

Epiphany

Shortly after this reconnection I had a dream—a powerhouse of a dream—quite a statement from one who by that time had several years of Jungian analysis:

> I stood downhill from a line of magnificent looking horses, watching them steadily make their way down a narrow, winding path carved into the sides of the foothills to the mountains towering behind them.
>
> It was night, and though it was dark when objects appear only in shades of black and gray I could clearly see colors: the bright green of the grass, the vibrant hues of the many mountain flowers and other foliage covering the slopes. What stood out the most were the glossy coats of the horses.

There was an order to their movements and each horse moved smoothly within that order, travelling the rough terrain more swiftly than horses would have done in waking life. They were lined up by color: blacks, grays, whites, sorrels, pintos, piebalds, paints, bays, duns, buckskins and palominos. I was filled with awe at the resplendency of these horses I have never seen equaled in either dreams or waking states. If there was an end to the line it wasn't visible to me.

They passed so close I could have reached out to touch each one. Then one horse pulled out of line and stood next to me. His coat was a lighter color than the horses currently in view. Together we watched the passing parade of horses for some time. He frequently spoke to me, each time turning to look me full in the face as he did. Then he was gone.

I recognized the path the horses took in the dream as one that threaded through the high mountain meadows and foothills behind the ranch. It would be convenient to say the horse that joined me for a while was Tank but I can't be sure. I have, however, come to believe that the rich dreams I had in childhood of horses speaking to me heralded the arrival of Tank and the healing role he would play in my life. So horses have indeed spoken to me.

My dream also jarred him loose, freeing him from the shadows of my heart where he had haunted me all those years. From that point on I never pushed him away when he surfaced. In fact, I opened to him as a flower to the sun, welcoming him and wanting to remember and embrace as much as possible about him. Memories of him sequestered for decades tumbled onto the pages. I eagerly wrote them down as they arrived—a jumble of so many experiences and adventures, not immediately seeing how they were connected.

I was amazed to see in retrospect the dangers we faced together and the developing bond we shared. Eventually, remembrances of experiences and events painful for me to acknowledge also surfaced, mercifully downloading at a stage in my life when I'd developed the maturity and accompanying capacity to face my pain and guilt about dropping him at the end of my second summer.

Now looking through a lens of a more expanded accumulation of knowledge about horses, I'm relieved to realize I hadn't hurt Tank. He hadn't felt rejected by my turning him in for a new model. He was a horse and his hierarchy of needs was well met. He was still part of the ranch herd, he had plenty to eat, and he was treated well. He'd been fine being with his new girl. She was nice to him. Nothing major had actually changed for him.

So, did he like me? Clearly he did. His ways of demonstrating that were evident to me and others. Was I special to him? Again—yes, I think so, but in horse terms, not human ones. To him I was probably something similar to what the alfalfa field was to him—really cool to have around and have access to. Did he miss me? Maybe in his way, but he would not have longed for me the way I did for him. And nothing he may have felt about my disappearance from his life would be close to the anguish he would have felt if he'd been separated from the herd.

But then the night of that wild storm he had invited me back into his life ...

I love Tank even more today because the completion of the deep necessity to write this story gave me a better understanding of the exceptional nature of his being, what he and I experienced that was larger than the two of us, and the ability to see my patterns by seeing what went on between us.

Recently a scene appeared in one of my regular meditations. It came into focus slowly. I recognized it as a particular mountain meadow we frequently rode in behind the ranch, above the path the horses in my dream took in their trek down the mountain and into my consciousness. I'm sitting in the upper-most portion of the meadow. Over waves of tall grass rippling in the wind I see a small cluster of boulders a little ways downhill. There's something taking shape next to them and I see it's a horse, its pale coat lightly tinged with red. I walk toward it and see it's Tank. He turns to look at me, chewing a mouthful of the long grass, some of it sticking out of both sides of his mouth.

As I get closer I realize *it is Tank*—not just a representation of him but we are again meeting on the same plane we sometimes inhabited together beyond our present time. *It's really him!* I actually smell him, touch him, feel the warmth of his big solid body, feel the veins on his shoulder, neck and head and trace them, my fingertips knowing where they are before they reach them. I twist my fingers in his mane and feel its smooth, wiry hairs. His left ear cocks toward me as I talk to him. I gently stroke the soft velvet of his ears and scratch around their base. I put my ear next to his cheek and listen to him chew. I bury my face in his neck and start to sob, getting a mouthful of mane, so grateful for this remarkable gift of his big, gentle, wise presence once again.

So once more Tank and I transcended a linear timeline. Now instead of saying, as I have most of my life, that the last time I was with Tank was August of 1959, I can say I most recently was with him June of 2011. This gives me something to look forward to the next time, whenever and on whatever plane that may be, because I know we are not really separated.

Epilogue

Connecting the seen with the unseen worlds

Tank was the first living being I consciously shared "other world" experiences with on a plane infinitely broader and more knowing than the one we daily inhabited. He was the first in a long line of people, and a few animals, with whom I would realize this connection. Like some sort of equine "familiar," Tank was with me in all such experiences I had at the ranch, if not as an active participant at least in my presence. And, as with any key emotional or transitional happening, we never forget who was first to go there with us which adds to the feeling of specialness I feel for him.

I have come to recognize there is a bridge between our seen and unseen worlds. Across it flow guidance and direction that are at work in our lives, sometimes in remarkable and startling ways. I know this and increasingly rely on it. I just can't prove it exists other than through my own experience.

For instance, I will never know specifically what it was that pushed me to the ground to save me from being crushed by the boulder. I will never know what made Tank "rip the reins out of our hands" at the top of that cliff to decide for us not only where we needed to go, but to smash a trail through the brush to get us there. Nor will I know why Tank chose to situate the two of us in front of the graves he did—because he was the one who not only placed us there but kept us there in stillness.

Some of the ways I regularly nurture the linkage between these two worlds is by applying my inspirations to my skills as a poet and writer, also while moving closer to the outer margins of culture as an astrologer, helping other people see their connections to their seen and unseen worlds and the greater purposes of life revealed there.

And it was dreams and their mysterious origins in the unseen world that first brought magical horses to me, carrying messages I could not retrieve as a young child. But when I thought I had lost forever my real-life special horse, Tank, he was brought back to me 50 years later by the same magical dream horses. Together they enabled me to write this special story. So their messages have gotten through.

The trail heads home

I recently researched the source of the song "I Ride an Old Paint." I found that the poet Carl Sandburg rescued it from its now-impossible-to-trace roots in the Old West and made it available in more modern times. He described it this way: "There is rich poetry in the image of the rider so loving a horse he begs when he dies his bones shall be tied to his horse and the two of them sent wandering with their faces turned west."

Amen, Carl. That's what I hope Tank and I do the next time we meet on that common plane we've shared out of present time, out of present place. Because the trail never ends. It just keeps going to new places and revisiting old ones for the opportunity to see with new eyes, and sometimes we get to go with those we love very much—over and over.

www.ingramcontent.com/pod-product-compliance
Lightning Source LLC
LaVergne TN
LVHW041201080426
835511LV00006B/702